I WISH I WAITED FOR YOU
DIVORCED
And No Longer Willing to Settle

JESSIKA M. TATE

I Wish I Waited For You:
Divorced, and No Longer Willing to Settle

by Jessika M. Tate, Copyright ©2024

ISBN-13: 978-947288-77-5

All rights reserved solely by the author. The author certifies that except where designated, all contents are original and do not infringe upon the legal rights of any other person or work. No part of this book may be reproduced in any form without the permission of the author and the publisher.

Except where designated, all Scripture quotations are taken from the Holy Bible, the King James Version. Scripture quotations marked KJ21 are taken from the 21st Century King James Version®, copyright© 1994. Used by permission of Deuel Enterprises, Gary, SD 57237. All rights reserved. Scripture quotations marked NIV are taken from the New International Version®, NIV®. Copyright © 1973, 1978, 1984, 2011 by Biblica, Inc.™ Used by permission of Zondervan. All rights reserved worldwide. www.zondervan.com.

Printed in the United States

10 9 8 7 6 5 4 3 2 1

Cover and interior design by: Legacy Design Inc.
Legacydesigninc@gmail.com
Published by
Life To Legacy, LLC
P.O. 1239
Matteson, IL 60443
708-272-4444
www.Life2Legacy.com
Life2legacybooks@att.net

TABLE OF CONTENTS

Dedication — Pg. 4

Introduction — Pg. 5

1. Willing to Settle — Pg. 7

2. Know Your Value — Pg. 17

3. Face Your Past and Heal — Pg. 27

4. Listen to the Holy Spirit Within You — Pg. 41

5. Sex — Pg. 51

6. The Unexpected Aftermath of Divorce — Pg. 59

7. Curses — Pg. 75

8. Final Thoughts — Pg. 87

About the Author — Pg. 89

DEDICATION

I want to dedicate this book to my Lord and Savior Jesus Christ. I want to thank my family and friends for always supporting and believing in me through the pursuit of all my endeavors. I also want to thank my Kingdom church family for all their prayers and constant words of encouragement.

INTRODUCTION

I Wish I Would Have Waited for You is a book I wish I would have read before I entered into a covenant of marriage that altered the direction of my life. Had I truly understood the power of a marriage covenant and what God intended for a marital covenant to represent in the earth, I would not have entered into it so haphazardly. I should have been honest about my own shortcomings and motives. I should have sought God's face and exercised the due diligence necessary to obtain the right information about my partner. Had I not let desperation dictate my direction, chances are my marriage would not have ended in divorce.

This book is a reflection of my personal process as well as others similarly situated as myself, who entered into a marriage covenant that eventually led to divorce. Divorce is not a pretty process. One, I thought I never would have experienced. But through that process, I learned so much about myself and the awesome responsibility and gravity that comes with being married. Whether you are single, divorced, or widowed, my desire is to help those who want to get married understand the downside of divorce while appreciating the upside of not settling too soon.

This book will give you practical knowledge through real-life scenarios I have experienced in my own relationships and encountered in my career as an attorney. As a bonus, I will also impart spiritual wisdom from the Scriptures. Waiting can seem like a curse, but *waiting* on God will renew your strength and save your life. After reading this book, I hope that you will take the time necessary to seek God's face for direction in every area of your life, especially if you are planning to get married.

CHAPTER ONE
Willing to Settle

If you asked the average person, "Are you willing to settle for less than what God has for you?" The answer would be a resounding, No! But somehow when it comes to romantic relationships, settling becomes a viable option. Settling in a relationship means being ready and willing to accept less than what you want or deserve, at the expense of staying in a relationship that is a bad one for you. So, how do you get to the point of settling in a relationship, you might ask? Invariably, the primary reason is loneliness.

As a divorce attorney as well as, a part-time Associate Municipal Judge, I have had an opportunity to counsel people from all walks of life while going through the divorce process. I often ask the question "Why did you settle for this relationship knowing it was wrong for you from the very beginning?" Although I hear many answers, the one consistent response I hear is, "I was tired of being alone." Experiencing loneliness is a real thing that can be a common denominator for many people to encounter because we all need and desire for human companionship. However, the key is not to allow those thoughts of loneliness to motivate you to start or stay in a relationship that is ultimately not healthy.

Of course, when you are in a state of loneliness, that is easier said than done. Hindsight is always 20/20. However, you should know your romantic relationship is headed for destruction if loneliness is the sole reason why you start and stay in a bad situation. Why, might you ask? Because the fear of being alone might cause you to ignore the usual red flags in a potential partner and cause you to settle for someone less than what God's best is for you. Red flags are warning signs that indicate unhealthy or toxic behavior in a partner. Some common red flags you see in relationships are partners with anger issues, overly controlling behavior, jealous tendencies, physical and emotional abuse, infidelity, and addiction issues.

To give you an example, let's say you are the type of person who doesn't typically stay in a relationship with someone who has a history of infidelity in the relationship. But because you're feeling lonely, you might overlook this fact and stay in a relationship with someone who cheats. What would then be the likely results of that decision if there is no change in their behavior? First your peace of mind would be diminished and your trust in them would erode. Now every time they leave your presence, or receive a call or text, you're disturbed by it wondering if they are attempting to hook up with someone else. Second, you could ignore the behavior and start making excuses for their cheating and dismiss your suspicions. Neither circumstance is God's best for you. However, there is a best situation out there waiting for you, but you must seek God's face first to find it. Nevertheless, many people stay in toxic relationships and compromise their wellbeing by ignoring those "obvious" red flags.

In addition to loneliness, there are many different reasons people may choose to settle when it comes to relationships. People may settle due to societal pressures, familiarity with the person, family pressures, financial motivations, emotional dependence, rejection, low self-esteem, denial, or a fear of abandonment. Now, this is not an exhaustive list of reasons on why people settle in relationships, but if you find you agree with any of these reasons mentioned above as a reason why you choose to start or stay in your current relationship, then you need to take the time to stop, reassess your motivations for being in that relationship, and make some better choices.

FOLLOWING THE PARENTAL MODEL

Initially, my motivation for getting married stemmed from my desire to have a long-term committed marriage like my parents. I grew up in a wholesome two-parent household. My parents were married thirty years at the time. I also watched my grandparents' marriage, and they were married fifty plus years. Although neither of those marriages were perfect, I was blessed to see them all love each other, forgive each other, and work through their differences to remain committed to achieving success in their marriages. As such, I always wanted to be married and achieve that same level of commitment in my own marriage, and I expected nothing less.

My grandmother married in her twenties, so turning 30 and being single for me in my family was not the norm, so I felt the pressure to conform to familial norms. I also felt the pressure to conform to societal norms that being single and over 30 was a problem, especially when I saw most of my friends my age that were already married or getting married. So, feeling like the odd ball, I tried keeping up with the proverbial Joneses—a pursuit that never ends well. Thus, 30 became my self-imposed deadline reinforced by familial and societal norms.

Comparing yourself to others can send you down the wrong path, which is what happened to me. I found myself for the first time in my life thinking I am willing to settle when it came to my romantic relationships, to accommodate my goal of marriage before 30. You may find yourself thinking that same thought that you are willing to settle too to accomplish marriage and if you are thinking that thought please know that you are not alone. However, you need to know that there are no legitimate reasons to settle for a relationship that is not the best God has in store for you. Instead of succumbing to any irrational reason to settle, you need to wait on the Lord before you make a life-long commitment to someone that is wrong for you.

Now, I do understand that society, especially social media, will make you feel like you are running out of time. We have all been guilty of scrolling on social media and seeing the images of the perfect couples (that really don't exist) in their happy relationships (that are actually fake), but cause you to think that waiting on God is not being realistic. One thing I had to realize is that people post the images on social media that they want you to see, which is often not what goes on in the relationship behind closed doors. You can't believe everything you see on social media. But what you can believe is the Word of God. In those moments of scrolling on social media, you must turn off the computer and your smartphone and open the Bible. This is how you will remember to hold onto what God's Word says about his promises for your future and believe God that He will do it for you. God is in control, not us. As such, there is no need to be desperate because God knows the plans He has for us regarding marriage in our lives, when, and how it will happen. I receive so much comfort in the following verse.

> *For I know the plans I have for you," declares the LORD, "plans to prosper you and not to harm you, plans to give you hope and a future. Jeremiah 29:11, NIV*

With God, there is always time left on the clock. The fight we have as Believers is to trust in the Lord and believe the Scriptures. When doubt enters in and tells us that our future is hopeless, that we are running out of time, and that marriage will never happen for us, we have to ask ourselves, "Whose report will you believe, doubt or the Lord?" Before I got married, I had those thoughts of fear and a lot more. I remember I had the fear of missing out on this storybook image of marriage if I didn't get married before 30. I always wanted and expected to have this handsome husband, two or more kids, a large home, and the white picket fence for my life. Although I eventually got married at 29, my marriage was anything but storybook. It was a nightmare. So, getting married before 30 didn't guarantee my marriage would be this "happily ever after" existence. I also had the fear of what people in society would think about me turning 30 and single. Would I be perceived as a failure despite all my professional accomplishments? That was a scary thought. Well, what about being 30 and divorced, an even scarier thought, but was now my reality. Looking back, I should have confronted those negative thoughts of fear in my single season, casted them down, and replaced them with positive thoughts of faith.

In 2 Corinthians 10:5 the Bible declares,

> *"Casting down imaginations, and every high thing that exalteth itself against the knowledge of God, and bringing into captivity every thought to the obedience of Christ."*

This is a powerful passage. According to the *Strong's Exhaustive Concordance of the Bible*, the phrase "casting down imaginations" originates from two Greek words *kathaireo* and *logismos*. Kathaireo means to *demolish* or *bring down*. Logismos, means *arguments* or *reasonings*. The Apostle Paul is urging Believers in this scripture to confront and dismantle every negative argument or thought pattern that opposes the knowledge of God, or what God has declared in His Word. Negative thoughts of fear are not of God. They must be *cast down* and *demolished* and replaced with positive thoughts of faith, or else, these negative thoughts will lead to bad decisions and result in negative actions.

WHAT IS FAITH?

Faith is not just believing in anything. No matter how hard you believe it, the tooth fairy is not real. However, in Hebrews 11, the Bible gives us a good working definition of faith.

> *"Now faith is the substance of things hoped for, the evidence of things not seen. Hebrews 11:1*

In the Bible, *faith* is a concept that means having a *strong belief, trust, and confidence in God in which there is no tangible proof.* Faith says I will get married one day, when fear says I will never get married. Faith says, I am right where I need to be in my life, when fear says I am running out of time. Faith says, I will see my single season as an opportunity for personal growth and development, when fear says I will see my single season as a punishment or a sign that something is wrong with me. Faith says, God can and will do marriage for me one day, when fear says God won't ever do marriage for me.

Again, when fear comes, you must dismantle those negative thoughts of fear, and replace them with positive thoughts of faith. Constant worrying, negative thinking, and anxiety about your marital future can take a toll on your emotional, physical, and spiritual health, so you must be willing to let the fear go, have faith in God, wait, run your own race, and not be bothered by who or what you see going on around you. Here is another great scripture that will arrest that nagging anxiety.

> *⁶ Do not be anxious about anything, but in every situation, by prayer and petition, with thanksgiving, present your requests to God. ⁷ And the peace of God, which transcends all understanding, will guard your hearts and our minds in Christ Jesus.*
>
> **Philippians 4:6-7, NIV**

THE POWER OF PRAYER

Prayer is so important to presenting our requests to God regarding our desires to be married. His peace, surpasses our own understanding on any problems or challenges that confront us. I have learned that you must stay in a place of prayer until there is a shift in your thought process and the peace of God takes over. The power is in the peace. When you feel His peace, then worry no more. That's why you should never give up! Pray without ceasing and believe God that it will happen for you.

During my single life, I often thought if God put the desire for marriage in my heart, then why would He withhold marriage from me? From my perspective I thought I was ready to get married. Boy, did I need a reality check. Why, might you ask? Because before I got married, I did not know my value in God. I had failed to seek God's face in prayer to understand what God intended for marriage to be in the earth realm and how I was to play a role in that to accomplish his purpose for it. Also, I needed more time to work on my personal issues. The reason why so many problems arise in marriage is because we are the ones who bring the problems to the marriage. Problems do not just wish away when you say "I do." If not dealt with they get worse. I could not be the best that I could be in the marriage, because I had not dealt with my personal problems. Neither did my ex-husband. To this we both contributed and that brought an end to the marriage. However, divorce does not have to be an end to your marriage. You must trust God today to see the things you don't see and to advise you on what personal problems you need to work on before marriage. Trust is defined as a *firm belief in the reliability, truth, ability, or strength in something.* Trust in God for your future today and let Him direct your paths towards the godly marriage you desire.

TRUST

> *Trust in the LORD with all thine heart; and lean not unto thine own understanding. In all thy ways acknowledge him, and he shall direct thy paths. Proverbs 3:5-6*

Let me be the first to admit this, but *trust* can be a difficult proposition, but you can do it. You can learn from my mistakes. What does trusting in God for your marriage look like? It looks like letting go of your perception of how and when you think marriage should happen in your life. The timing, the specifics, the person, all of it. Letting go and letting God direct the paths and seasons of your life can be difficult to do. But consider this, God is the creator of the universe, and He knows all things, which means He knows every season of your life, including when your season to marry has arrived. Therefore, you must adopt the virtue of being patient because you do not want to do anything before the time or the season. As a result, you must master being content in the season you are now in, so you won't settle for an out of season marriage. God's best for you comes in the season He has planned for you. Remember the marriage that God has in store for you is the best and it is blessed. God designed marriage to be a divine covenant between a man and a woman on Earth.

> *Therefore they are no more two, but one flesh. What therefore God hath joined together, let not man put asunder." Matthew 19:6, KJ21*

"To be put asunder," is a biblical concept that means *to set aside*. God intended marriage to last forever and not to be set aside by any man. God never intended marriage to be entered into on a trial basis. Marriage is a life-long commitment between a man and a woman. However, society has made it almost normal to jump in and out of marriages like a game of hopscotch. They say fifty percent of first-time marriages end in divorce. Sixty percent of second-time marriages end in divorce. These are alarming statistics that you do not want to find yourself numbered among. Therefore, get it right the first time. Don't be willing to settle for less, when God has what is best waiting for you.

CHAPTER TWO
Know Your Value

It is imperative that you know your value before you enter a divine covenant of marriage. I believe when you know your value it makes you less willing to settle for less than the best for you. Remember God said, "I know the plans I have for you." In His plans is a dynamic, fruitful and fulfilling marriage, as well as other great things in other areas of your life. What does God's Word say about your value? Here are a few Scriptures to answer that question.

> *But ye are a chosen generation, a royal priesthood, an holy nation, a peculiar people; that ye should shew forth the praises of him who hath called you out of darkness into his marvellous light. 1 Peter 2:9*
>
> *I will praise thee; for I am fearfully and wonderfully made: marvellous are thy works; and that my soul knoweth right well. Psalm 139:14*

God says we are a royal priesthood, so we are kings and queens in His sight. As royalty, we should be treated as such. So why would we accept being treated like peasants? People will only treat you the way you allow them to treat you. During my single season, I completely forgot what God said about my value. I found myself in relationships where I was being told I was not as attractive as any of the other girls they had dated. My self-esteem was often assaulted because I was constantly told I was not good enough. Emotionally, I was so stressed because I was being repeatedly put down.

Many days I felt no more value than gum stuck to the bottom of someone's shoe. Yet, I chose to stay in these types of relationships time and time again because I forgot my value as a queen. Although I grew up in a household with two parents that fostered an environment of high self-esteem, due to years of rejection in my adult life from these past romantic relationships, I developed low self-esteem. Before I got married, God knew this issue of low self-esteem had developed a weakness in me, but I didn't know it because I failed to seek God's face in prayer to reveal that truth to me.

Low self-esteem was a weakness that I needed to address and work on before I got married, but I did not. Because I did not, my marriage only exacerbated this weakness that needed to be dealt with. Do you know what weaknesses lie inside of you that need to be dealt with? Let's be honest here, everyone has weaknesses and shortcomings they need to work on. The key is to identify those weaknesses and take a conscious approach to address them. After my divorce, I identified my issue with low self-esteem. I took steps to rebuild confidence in myself. First, I had to get rid of all the distractions in my life and get into the Word of God. Through prayer, I sought God's face to learn what He said about my true value. Secondly, by faith I had to walk in the assurance of truth. Once my spiritual eyes were opened, I could see the mistreatment in my relationships and I decided that behavior was no longer acceptable to me.

FROM TRAUMA TO TRIUMPH

During my life, I have met many people who have shared similar stories. The following is an account of a lady who told me her triumphant testimony. This woman had gotten married very young to her first love but her husband turned out to be physically and emotionally abusive. Year after year, she had hoped he would get counseling for his anger, and he would often promise to do so, but never would follow through. She recounted how he could be so sweet and charming to others in public but was a hellion to her behind closed doors. Walking around on eggshells was a common occurrence by her to not incite his anger and rage. There were times when he would physically abuse her, and leave bruises that she had to explain away to her friends and family.

After his bouts of physical abuse, he would come home with lavish gifts like diamond necklaces and other jewelry begging forgiveness and promising to change for the better. This lady accepted the years of abuse because it became their norm. After twenty years of marriage, she found out that he had an extramarital affair, which became the last straw of disrespect for her. Through counseling, prayer, and family support, she realized her value in God was so much more than what she had allowed him to treat her over the years. She divorced him, got healed and delivered from all that emotional pain and trauma. Years later she remarried and is living a life free of abuse no longer allowing any person to treat her less than what God says she is valued.

When you don't know your value in God, you open the door for someone else to valuate you according to their standards. You *do not* deserve to be abused or treated like a dog. No amount of apologies or nice gifts can take away the physical and emotional bruises an abuser leaves behind. You have too much value to be mistreated by anyone. Too often I hear my divorced clients say they saw the red flags before they got married like anger issues from their spouse or bad spending habits, but they chose to ignore those red flags for the sake of the relationship. Red flags should never be ignored because they are signs of significant problems. At the end of the day, remember you are God's child. He did not create you to be abused but to be loved and appreciated. You are beautiful and unique, and you do not deserve mistreatment from anyone, especially your spouse.

There are many misconceptions about marriage, some being that marriage will solve all your problems or that marriage shouldn't be hard work if you love each other. Believing in these misconceptions can lead your marriage down a path to destruction. I know I had the misconception that I needed marriage in order to become fulfilled or content in my life. I thought I needed a husband to make me feel happy in some way. Boy, was my perception off. Instead of focusing on my husband to do everything to make me happy, I needed to learn how to cultivate happiness within myself. I remember one day, years after my divorce, my spiritual mom said to me so calmly while I was crying in her home about the loss of my ex-husband, "you act like he was the prize." I remember being speechless after hearing those words because it was true. After all these years, I had been so focused on my ex-husband's perceived value and what I thought I lost that I didn't understand my own value as the wife. I completely missed the fact that as his wife I was the prize all along and that I could feel happy with or without him. Please don't make the same mistake that I did. Wives, please know you have significant value in marriage.

> *Whoso findeth a wife findeth a good thing, and obtaineth favour of the LORD. Proverbs 18:22*

When we got married, my ex-husband found a good thing and obtained favor of the Lord because I was the favor. Favor is defined as *approval, support, or liking for someone or something*. In the verses that follow, King Solomon so poetically writes about *the virtuous woman*.

> [10] *Who can find a virtuous woman? for her price is far above rubies.*
> [11] *The heart of her husband doth safely trust in her, so that he shall have no need of spoil.*
> [12] *She will do him good and not evil all the days of her life.*
> [13] *She seeketh wool, and flax, and worketh willingly with her hands.*

¹⁴ She is like the merchants' ships; she bringeth her food from afar.
¹⁵ She riseth also while it is yet night, and giveth meat to her household, and a portion to her maidens.
¹⁶ She considereth a field, and buyeth it: with the fruit of her hands she planteth a vineyard.
¹⁷ She girdeth her loins with strength, and strengtheneth her arms.
¹⁸ She perceiveth that her merchandise is good: her candle goeth not out by night.
¹⁹ She layeth her hands to the spindle, and her hands hold the distaff.
²⁰ She stretcheth out her hand to the poor; yea, she reacheth forth her hands to the needy.
²¹ She is not afraid of the snow for her household: for all her household are clothed with scarlet.
²² She maketh herself coverings of tapestry; her clothing is silk and purple.
²³ Her husband is known in the gates, when he sitteth among the elders of the land.
²⁴ She maketh fine linen, and selleth it; and delivereth girdles unto the merchant.
²⁵ Strength and honour are her clothing; and she shall rejoice in time to come.
²⁶ She openeth her mouth with wisdom; and in her tongue is the law of kindness.
²⁷ She looketh well to the ways of her household, and eateth not the bread of idleness.
²⁸ Her children arise up, and call her blessed; her husband also, and he praiseth her.
²⁹ Many daughters have done virtuously, but thou excellest them all.
³⁰ Favour is deceitful, and beauty is vain: but a woman that feareth the LORD, she shall be praised.

> *³¹ Give her of the fruit of her hands; and let her own works praise her in the gates. Proverbs 31:10-31*

For a marriage to be successful, wives not only need to know their value, but husbands need to appreciate how valuable she is and vice versa. Husbands have significant value in marriage. A husband's role is to lead the household with love, honor, and integrity. Leading does not mean being a dictator or abusive, but being the head of the family God's way. Godly husbands lead by example in the areas of love, honor, and integrity, providing a spiritual covering for the family and the home. He guides the relationship in the direction that provides the best results for both partners. The husband is the head of the wife and is the spiritual leader of the household. As the husband follows Christ, the wife follows the husband, which is the spiritual order of a godly marriage.

In the following passage, the role of the godly husband is delineated.

> *²¹ and be subject to one another in the fear of Christ. ²² Wives, be subject to your own husbands, as to the Lord. ²³ For the husband is the head of the wife, as Christ also is the head of the church, He Himself being the Savior of the body. ²⁴ But as the church is subject to Christ, so also the wives ought to be to their husbands in everything. ²⁵ Husbands, love your wives, just as Christ also loved the church and gave Himself up for her, ²⁶ so that He might sanctify her, having cleansed her by the washing of water with the word, ²⁷ that He might present to Himself the church in all her glory, having no spot or wrinkle or any such thing; but that she would be holy and blameless. ²⁸ So husbands ought also to love their own wives as their own bodies. He who loves his own wife loves himself; ²⁹ for no one ever hated his own flesh, but nourishes and cherishes it, just as Christ also does the church, ³⁰ because we are members of His body. ³¹ For this reason a man*

> *shall leave his father and mother and shall be joined to his wife, and the two shall become one flesh. ³² This mystery is great; but I am speaking with reference to Christ and the church. ³³ Nevertheless, each individual among you also is to love his own wife even as himself, and the wife must see to it that she respects her husband. Ephesians 5:21-33*

There are many benefits to a godly marriage. One such benefit is that godly husbands love their wives as they love themselves and godly wives respect their husbands. When it comes to marriage, husbands need their wives to respect them, and wives need their husbands to love them. What is respect? Respect is a strong feeling of admiration for someone elicited by their abilities, qualities, and achievements. What is love? In 1 Corinthians 13:4-7, we get the Bible's definition.

> *⁴ Love is patient, love is kind. It does not envy, it does not boast, it is not proud. ⁵ It does not dishonor others, it is not self-seeking, it is not easily angered, it keeps no record of wrongs. ⁶ Love does not delight in evil but rejoices with the truth. ⁷ It always protects, always trusts, always hopes, always perseveres. NIV*

Part of understanding your value is knowing how you express and receive love which involves the dynamic of what Gary Chapman identifies as the "love languages." In his book *The Five Love Languages,* there are five primary ways we give and receive love; (1) affirmation, (2) quality time, (3) receiving gifts, (4) acts of service, and (5) physical touch. For me, my main love languages are *affirmation and quality time.* I receive love by words of encouragement and kindness, words of acceptance, and by spending quality time with my partner. My life can be very busy, so spending quality time for me in a romantic relationship consists of sitting at home together watching a movie or going on vacation anywhere just the two of us. The idea here is quality, not quantity. Your love language could be receiving gifts wherein you receive love by receiving gifts by your partner, no matter how big or small, because the value is seen in the thought behind giving the gift. Or your love language could be acts of service wherein you receive love from your partner by them doing activities for you that make your life easier or more enjoyable.

It is important to know what your love language is. Why, might you ask? Because God made us all unique so you can't assume that we all have the same love language. Your love language may be different from your partner's. At the end of the day, we all want our love tanks to be full and to be loved by our partner in a way that we need to receive it. If you do not receive love the way you need to, your love tank will be empty, and you will find yourself emotionally dying in the relationship and destined for divorce. Nobody wants that result. As such, it is important to know what your language is and be willing to communicate that love language to your partner.

Once that love language is communicated, if your partner wants the relationship to be the best it can be, they will make the adjustments to love you the way that works for you. If your partner is unwilling or unable to make the adjustments necessary to give you love the way you say you need to receive it, then you must run fast away from the relationship. You must accept the truth that it is possible this person does not have the capacity to love you the way you need to be loved and that you need to wait for the one that does.

So many times, I have met with people in my office going through a divorce and have been told they did not feel loved or respected by their significant other. I remember one wife telling me she felt like her husband just tolerated her in the relationship. He would rather spend all his time at work making money or hanging out with the boys after work ended instead of spending any quality time at home with her. Why did this become an issue for her? Because her love language was quality time, which meant quality time was how she received love from her husband.

Year after year would pass and the wife saw that the husband was not making the necessary adjustments to spend more quality time with her. They even went to counseling to work through the issue and identify ways for the husband to set aside quality time in his week to spend with his wife. Even after the counseling, this couple still ended up in my office, headed for divorce, because the husband refused to change. A godly marriage is worth the wait because the partner orchestrated by Him for you will be willing and able to make the adjustments necessary to give you the love the way you need to receive it. Another benefit of a God directed and selected marriage is the power of agreement. This is a biblical concept that can be found in the Gospel of Matthew. Jesus declared,

> *"...truly I tell you that if two of you on earth agree about anything they ask for, it will be done for them by my Father in heaven." Matthew 18:19, NIV*

When two people come together as one mind, and seek God's face in prayer, they can ask anything together according to His will, and God will do it for them. Agreement does not mean you always see things the exact same way, but it is the willingness of the two people to get on the same page and work together as one mind, one will, and one emotion to achieve a common goal. It is called unity.

A godly marriage, through the power of agreement, can cause prosperity in dimensions we have never seen before because two people in prayer can ask God for increase after increase and God will give them what they ask of Him. Two people in a marriage, who are willing to submit themselves one to another, having grace for each other's faults, can be a safe place for the other person to grow in their purpose and destiny. Your spouse can be the yin to your yang, sort of speak, knowing how to pick up the pieces you don't know how to pick up. Given all the benefits of marriage, God never designed marriage to end in divorce. Yet, divorce can be your reality when you are willing to settle.

CHAPTER THREE
Face Your Past and Heal

Healing was definitely a long journey for me, however, everyone's healing journey is different. I wish I could tell you healing is super easy, and to not worry about it if you need healing, because healing would be easy for you too, but I would be lying. Healing takes a lot of work. One person, it could take ten days to heal from an issue and another person ten years to heal from that same issue. Divorce is the type of situation that requires a lot of healing in your mental health.

My divorce was the most painful experience in my life. I was completely heartbroken and emotionally distraught for many years after my divorce, because despite my motivations for getting married, I loved my ex-husband. I wanted our marriage to work, and I wanted us both to be the best versions of ourselves and defy the naysayers that said our marriage wouldn't last. After the divorce, I had to process all these emotional wounds. On the outside, I appeared fine, but on the inside, I was dying emotionally.

Emotional wounds are traumatic experiences that cause deep pain to a person on a psychological and/or mental level. Some common emotional wounds are rejection, abandonment, betrayal, or humiliation. Unlike physical wounds, emotional wounds lack visible scars, which makes them a lot harder to see and treat. Physical wounds are a lot easier to see and treat. For example, if you fall off a bicycle and break your leg, you can see the bone sticking out from the skin or the bleeding in the area of injury. You wouldn't see those injuries and keep trying to walk around on that broken leg. No, you would immediately call for help and seek medical attention from a doctor. Afterward, the doctor would perform surgery to fix your leg and stitch up the surface injuries. The doctor would send you home with medicine for the pain and place you in a cast to protect your leg from further injury. It is easy to see and understand this process of healing. But it is not so easy to see and understand the process of healing from pain with emotional wounds because those wounds are invisible and psychological. Emotional wounds are very real and the grief that accompanies them are different for everyone.

For me, during my process of healing after the divorce, I found it hard to forgive myself for divorcing, hard to forgive my ex-husband for being a willing participant in the demise of our marriage, and hard to forgive God for allowing the divorce to happen. Why didn't I wait on God was the nagging question that played repeatedly in my mind. In order to move forward and heal, I had to find the answer to that question through deep introspection and face my past.

FORGIVE GOD

First, I had to forgive God. I was so angry with God for allowing my divorce to happen. Although, I was the one that decided to enter this marriage with this man, I could not understand why God in all his great splendor and infinite wisdom allowed me to marry this man in the first place knowing it would end in divorce. What I failed to realize is that God didn't hold a gun to my head and make me marry this man. I did so of my own free will and I had to accept responsibility for my decision to do so.

Before I got married, I knew the relationship with my ex-husband was toxic, but I loved him, so I always hoped that God would give my ex-husband this Damascus road experience like Paul had in the Book of Acts, where one day my ex-husband would see the light, recognize my value as his wife, and then treat me the way I wanted and needed to be treated. Well that never happened, so I blamed God and turned my heart away from him. Please do not be like me and make that mistake. Blaming God or anyone else for your decisions is problematic and can only lead you down a path of denial. Besides, our displeasure or anger with God won't get you anywhere. We are the ones that need God, not the other way around.

Taking responsibility for your actions is an important part of emotional healing. It involves owning up to the positive and negative consequences of your choices and behavior, rather than attributing them to any person or anything else. I know that is easier said than done, because the world teaches us to point fingers at anyone or anything else but ourselves when bad things happen. But you will find that a change to your perspective can be the key to you moving forward after an emotional wound has been suffered. It was that way for me. My mind needed to be renewed. Here is one of my favorite scriptures on renewal of your mind.

> *"And be not conformed to this world: but be ye transformed by the renewing of your mind, that ye may prove what is that good, and acceptable, and perfect, will of God." Romans 12:2*

There are many ways to go about getting a renewed mind or more simply put, a change in perspective. Many people will seek the advice of God, family, friends, coaches, mentors, or even a licensed therapist to help change their perspective. The key is to ask for help! I know it is not always easy to ask for help, but when you are dealing with emotional wounds and trauma, all you want is relief.

After my divorce, because I was mad at God, I didn't seek advice from him. I did have enough sense to know I still needed help to process the emotional trauma, so I sought advice from trusted family members and friends that I knew would challenge my perspective and offer contrary viewpoints. I knew surrounding myself with "yes" men or women would hinder my healing progress moving forward, so I had to distance myself from those people and surround myself with people that would tell it like it is. I also began seeing a licensed therapist. I know there is still a stigma in our culture around going to therapy. That stigma often leads people to avoid seeking professional help, but mental health deserves the same attention as physical health. There is no shame in asking for professional help. I did and therapy helped me change my perspective.

After many counseling sessions, I was able to see the role I played in the demise of my marriage. I had to acknowledge the fact I saw red flags and that multiple times God created ways of escape for me before I got married, but I chose to ignore them all and push forward. That was all on me, not God. Once I accepted responsibility and no longer blamed God for the divorce, I was finally able to turn and ask Him heal my emotional wounds, including my broken heart. Being brokenhearted is the time to turn to God, not away from God. Thankfully God stays close to the brokenhearted and heals them. This was King David's testimony in the Psalms when he wrote,

> *"The LORD is close to the brokenhearted and saves those who are crushed in spirit." Psalm 34:18, NIV*

> *"And He heals the brokenhearted and binds up their wounds." Psalm 147:3, NIV*

So often I hear people say time heals all wounds. Well, that's a lie. After my divorce, the years went by and by, and I was still just as hurt and mad as I was the day I got divorced. It was not until I forgave God and asked Him in prayer to heal my broken heart. That's when the true process of my healing began. If you are brokenhearted and you don't know where to start in prayer, a good prayer to say to God during your prayer time is, "God, I need you to help me. I can't do this without you. Please fill every broken place in my heart with your love and peace. Come rescue me because I'm hurting. I need you right now."

Once I forgave God, I prayed similar prayers during my prayer time. I would often cry my eyes out completely sobbing in emotional pain. Pray and cry, pray and cry, and pray and cry some more. It seemed like a never-ending cycle of praying and crying. Eventually, I got to the point in prayer where I was able to not only cry to God about the situation, but I was ready and willing to listen to God for His response. Whatever that was; the good, the bad, and the ugly. It was only then when I heard God's voice reveal to me that there was purpose in my pain.

The Bible declares,

> *"And we know that all things work together for good to them that love God, to them who are the called according to his purpose" Romans 8:28*

The scripture says all things work together for good. Does that scripture include a broken heart? Yes, even a broken heart God can work together for good. Surely, that scripture doesn't include a divorce, I used to think. Yes, even a divorce can work together for good. I came to realize that God never wanted me to be divorced but God did allow my divorce to happen in hoping that I would learn from it, not make the same mistake again, and press forward to receive the best he has in store for me. There is purpose in your pain. You might not see that now. I know I didn't see it for years, but now I know that God can use your pain to help somebody else. I sure hope this book is doing that for you. Allow God to heal you from the pains of your past. He will do it if you let him.

FORGIVE MYSELF

Once I was able to forgive God, the next thing was to forgive myself for the divorce. Naturally, I am a very private person, so I don't usually let people see into any areas of my private life. But, in this situation, I had this huge public wedding, invited all the dignitaries, and put our whole relationship on public display. I brought this person around my family and friends and demanded from them that he be immediately accepted without any reproof. I put the stamp, "This is God," on our relationship and I didn't allow anyone, including God, to say anything different. Given that I had built a pretty successful public/professional life, the expectation for me was that I would build nothing less than a long successful marriage in my private life no matter who I was married to. So, when I got divorced less than one year after I got married, I felt the public shame and humiliation that soon followed from my decision to marry this individual. People knew that I had spent all this money on a wedding and the marriage didn't even last a year. I was so ashamed and disappointed in myself that I didn't wait to marry the best God had for me. I saw myself as a failure. Failure is defined as a lack of success or the inability to meet an expectation. In order to move forward in the healing process, I came to realize that I was not a failure. I needed to renew my mind and change my perception. Although the marriage failed, I was not a failure.

> *And be not conformed to this world: but be ye transformed by the renewing of your mind, that ye may prove what is that good, and acceptable, and perfect, will of God. Romans 12:2*

Although the world views divorce as a failure, sometimes divorce can be deliverance. Deliverance is defined *as the action of being rescued or set free.* There are times in my practice as a divorce attorney where I have advised people that were in emotionally and physically abusive relationships to file for divorce. Abuse is used as a tactic in relationships to manipulate and have power over an individual. I remember one lady that came into my office about a divorce her husband had filed against her. When I talked with her, she told me that she loved her husband and that she didn't want to get a divorce. Although her husband had committed infidelity during the marriage, because she loved him, she kept forgiving him after each affair, which was more than one, and they stayed together despite his lack of commitment to repairing the relationship. Year after year, he would tell her he was not sexually attracted to her, which is a common form of emotional abuse. Instead of the husband looking inward to resolve his own issues with self-esteem, possible childhood pain on why he would be so comfortable to cheat in the first place, he would rather blame the wife for having the affairs citing the lack of sexual intimacy between them. It had gotten to the point that he began mistreating her, withholding affection, and calling her names where the wife ultimately felt devalued by him, ugly, and worthless. The husband just didn't want her anymore and it was time for the wife to accept that fact and sign the divorce papers. In this case, her divorce was deliverance.

Another example where I saw divorce can be deliverance, I remember one guy who came to me for a consultation about a divorce, his wife hadn't had sexual relations with him for over a year and he was a very young guy. His wife was no longer physically attractive to him for whatever reason, so she emotionally and physically checked out of the marriage having decided she was not willing to change or seek help to try to change. They only remained in the relationship together for the sake of the children. This guy was a very fun, happy, go-lucky, extrovert kind of guy, and the stress he felt from the sexless marriage was starting to turn him into a bitter old man. He didn't want to be unfaithful to his wife, but he found himself contemplating having an affair to meet his sexual needs, something he vowed he would never do.

As he talked with me, I watched his demeanor become more and more depressive as he emotionally beat himself up due to feeling hurt about the situation and the decision he had made to get divorced. I could literally see the hurt in his eyes, and I could hear the hurt in his voice when he talked. He stated to me how he felt like he was losing the fun, happy-go-lucky, extrovert kind of person he was before he got married and, was he right. But the guilt he felt behind his desire not to stay in a marriage that was hurting him was weighing him down. What he needed at this point was deliverance.

I have found that beating yourself up is not going to change or fix the situation. A vital step in the healing and deliverance process is accepting you were hurt and forgiving yourself for allowing someone else to hurt you. The emotional pain happened, no matter who was at fault, and you were hurt. That is a fact that cannot be changed and must be dealt with. The key is to not allow that hurt to take over your life. The enemy is good at playing your hurts and mistakes in your mind like a broken record over and over again. Don't give the enemy space to keep doing just that because beating yourself up is only going to make you feel more depressed and suicidal.

The suicide rate for those who are divorced or separated is twice as high as the suicide rate for those who are married. Why, might you ask? Because the enemy can make you feel like the pain of divorce or separation will never end and that you have no way out of the pain, which is not true. With God, there is always a way of escape out of the pain. You can be healed and experience deliverance. The pain of divorce or separation can come to an expected end, and I am a witness to that, but you must choose to undergo a process of healing, which includes forgiving yourself. Forgiving yourself requires that you extend to yourself grace and mercy because you are not perfect. Only God is perfect. You are capable of making mistakes. Some mistakes are worse than others. The key is when a mistake has been made, to accept it happened, learn from it, let it go, and move forward.

Fame theologian Reinhold Niebuhr wrote the following serenity prayer, "God, grant me the serenity to accept the things I cannot change, the courage to change the things I can, and the wisdom to know the difference." Boy, do we need wisdom to know the difference. A characteristic of wisdom is the ability to judge what is right, true, or lasting. The good thing is God gives wisdom to those who ask for wisdom. All you need to do is ask.

"If any of you lacks wisdom, you should ask God, who gives generously to all without finding fault, and it will be given to you. James 1:5, NIV

FORGIVE MY EX-HUSBAND

Lastly, I had to forgive my ex-husband. Baby, this was the hardest one. Why, might you ask? Because we said vows to each other in front of God and everyone! We vowed through sickness and health and to death do us part. Now, we are divorced. Wait a minute, wait a minute, wait a minute. What about my happy ending? Divorce, how is that fair? The demise of my marriage was like a bad movie with endless sequels. I remembered every detail of every bad scene that happened between us. I had built a case against my ex-husband for all the things I thought he had done wrong to me over the course of our relationship. The problem was that I believed my case was valid, so I extended to him no grace, no mercy, and I wouldn't let my case go. You may think it hurts the other party to hold on to your case, but I promise you it only hurts you.

Given the level of emotional pain and trauma I experienced because of my ex-husband, in order to become fully healed, I needed to set realistic expectations for my healing and deliverance process. Setting realistic expectations was a key component in the healing process. When we don't set realistic expectations, we can often end up disappointed and frustrated at ourselves, which in the long run doesn't help us heal. A common unrealistic expectation is that progress means we have to consistently be taking steps forward, which is not true. Sometimes, progress can mean two steps forward, one step backward, and then another step forward.

Many times, over the years, I had to encourage myself that I was progressing in my healing process of forgiving my ex-husband even though I took those steps backwards at times. Sometimes, I could see my ex-husband at a gas station or somewhere else out in public and could wave and speak to him without feeling any resentment in my heart. Then there were other times, I saw him out in public and he would see me, and I would purposely walk past him like the wind without acknowledging or speaking to him. In reality, I was feeling completely pissed off in my heart. Situations like this are real life moments and they happen to many people who go through a divorce. Taking steps backwards doesn't mean failure, it just means you need more time to heal. The key is to get back up when you fall and try again to move forward because God would want us to show love to those ones who we feel have done us wrong.

> *⁴³ "You have heard that it was said, 'Love your neighbor and hate your enemy.' ⁴⁴ But I tell you, love your enemies and pray for those who persecute you, ⁴⁵ that you may be children of your Father in heaven. He causes his sun to rise on the evil and the good, and sends rain on the righteous and the unrighteous. ⁴⁶ If you love those who love you, what reward will you get? Are not even the tax collectors doing that? ⁴⁷ And if you greet only your own people, what are you doing more than others? Do not even pagans do that? ⁴⁸ Be perfect, therefore, as your heavenly Father is perfect. Matthew 5:43-48, NIV*

Since my ex-husband had caused me so much emotional pain and suffering, it was difficult to show love or to even pray for him. In my mind, I had a reason to be angry with him, and my pride was not ready to let go of the resentment. You may have heard of the adage, "hurt people hurt people." It is true. I wanted to see him hurt as badly as I knew I was hurting. In spite of my hurt feelings, God would want me to show love. Not only to him but to anyone else that caused me pain. Why? Because God is love. So, not speaking to my ex-husband was not exhibiting God's love. Therefore, I had to let go of all my reasons to be angry at him so that I could experience deliverance and healing. I know many people may find themselves in that same situation, but you have to face the pains of your past and heal. If not, all the pain you feel may lead to the sin of unforgiveness. That is what happened to me. All the pain, regret, and anger I felt towards my ex-husband turned into unforgiveness. Unforgiveness is when you are unwilling to forgive someone who has offended or did a wrong against you. Holding on to unforgiveness, anger and malice, will hinder your own deliverance.

> *[14] For if you forgive other people when they sin against you, your heavenly Father will also forgive you. 15 But if you do not forgive others their sins, your Father will not forgive your sins. Matthew 6:14-15*

How could I ask God to forgive me for my sins when I was walking around full of the sin of unforgiveness in my heart concerning my ex-husband. Unforgiveness has physical consequences, which is a lesson I learned the hard way. Unforgiveness is like a spiritual cancer that destroys you from the inside out. When we hold onto unforgiveness, there are physiological symptoms that manifest in our body. Stress hormones are released which cause inflammation, which is linked to numerous health issues, including but not limited to heart disease, diabetes, certain cancers, and auto-immune diseases. Something I know now all too well.

In December 2019, out of nowhere, I became deathly ill. I went to doctor after doctor trying to figure out what was going on with me. I lost 40 pounds in a three-month time span, and I could no longer properly digest my food. After multiple surgeries, colonoscopies, pain, and anguish, I was finally diagnosed with Crohn's Disease in my late thirties. Crohn's disease is a type of inflammatory bowel disease. It causes swelling of the tissues (inflammation) in your digestive tract, which can lead to abdominal pain, severe diarrhea, fatigue, weight loss, and malnutrition. Please know I never had any symptoms of Crohn's Disease before this time. But, through the open door of unforgiveness, I became deathly ill, having all these symptoms, and had what the doctor called an acute onset of the disease, which means suddenly, out of nowhere.

It would be a four-year journey for me fighting for my life. April 20, 2022, I had a major surgery called an ileostomy that changed the way poop exited my body from my bowel to an opening made outside of my stomach, which required me to wear a colostomy bag. A fact I kept secret from many people. The physical pain in my body was out of this world at times. The pain medicine would barely make a dent to relieve my pain at times. If only I could have stayed at home in bed and suffered in silence, but no, I still had to run a law firm, still had to argue legal cases in court, and still had to try to live some sort of meaningful life through the onset of constant pain.

May 20, 2023, I went to a spiritual conference in Chicago hosted by iRoar Global, where I learned that the fruit of unforgiveness is the spirit of infirmity. Before that moment, I had never seen the connection between unforgiveness and my physical health. That day I realized that my unforgiveness was the source of my infirmity. That was an epiphany for me. It finally clicked. If you find yourself battling a health scare out of nowhere, this can be your "eureka" moment for you too. That day I realized holding on to the case I had against my ex-husband was not worth battling physical pain for the rest of my life. That day, by faith, I decreed and declared with my mouth that I forgive my ex-husband, and I repented for having any unforgiveness in my heart concerning him. Repent only means to turn from doing that sin and to do the sin no more.

> *If my people, which are called by my name, shall humble themselves, and pray, and seek my face, and turn from their wicked ways; then will I hear from heaven, and will forgive their sin, and will heal their land. 2 Chronicles 7:14*

In my situation, I had to turn from my wicked ways, which was the unforgiveness in my heart which acted as a curse against my physical body. Once I let go of my case and forgave my ex-husband from any offense that I felt he committed against me, God then heard my prayer for healing, forgave my sins and destroyed the yoke of bondage that had brought a curse on my life.

On June 23, 2023, I had my last surgery to reverse the physical affects this curse wrought in my body. I remember my doctor telling me before my surgery that the kind of surgery I was having had less than a ten percent chance of success. When he said that to me, I had no fear or doubt that the surgery would be a success, because I knew I had closed the door of unforgiveness by forgiving my ex-husband. So, with confidence I replied to him, "well looks like I am going to be part of that ten percent." Now, months after my surgery, that same doctor tells me I am a walking miracle. Praise God!

Although I am now completely healed from that infirmity, it does not mean that I escaped the consequences of my unforgiveness. Yes, please know that unforgiveness has consequences. One of those consequences is losing time. For me, I lost time. I spent four years of my life battling an illness in my body. That time could have been spent traveling or pursuing other personal and professional goals. Looking back, I could have spent that time working on becoming the best version of myself, so I could be in a better position to attract my next husband. Instead, that time was spent focused on battling daily physical pain, being in and out of hospitals, and numerous doctor's appointments. I would not wish that experience on anyone, so I beg you to not respond to emotional trauma like I did. Forgive, and forgive quickly.

Another unexpected consequence of my unforgiveness was the physical scars left on my body after the surgery. Every day when I take off my clothes and look in the mirror, I am reminded of the consequences of my unforgiveness. I see the thick two-inch horizontal scar on the right side of my stomach left from the surgery and the lasting imprint the colostomy bag left on my skin. For a while after my surgery, I questioned my attractiveness due to the scars. How would my beauty be perceived now by my new husband with these scars? God challenged me to renew my mind and change my perspective yet again. The enemy tried to kill me through the door of my unforgiveness, but God would not let it be so. My scars are a sign of my survival and victory over the enemy's plan. For that, my scars are beautiful, and any new husband of mine will see and appreciate that.

Again, praise God for my healing, but please know you don't have to be like me having to nearly die before you forgive. Offenses in relationships will come but learn how to forgive quickly and press forward to the best parts that God has in store for you in your life. Apostle Paul reminds us in the scripture below the importance of forgetting those things that are behind and straining towards what is ahead.

> ***Brothers and sisters, I do not consider myself yet to have taken hold of it. But one thing I do: Forgetting what is behind and straining toward what is ahead, [14] I press on toward the goal to win the prize for which God has called me heavenward in Christ Jesus. Philippians 3:13-14, NIV***

Your past is something to learn from, not something that is meant by God to weigh you down. Many people leave relationship after relationship brokenhearted experiencing emotional wounds without taking the time necessary to seek God's face and heal from the pains of their past. Don't be like many people. You have so much to look forward to when you face your past, heal, forgive, and then leave your past behind. If I can do it, you can too!

CHAPTER FOUR
Listen to the Holy Spirit Within You

Before you get married, you must take the time to stop and listen to the voice of the Holy Spirit within you to help guide you into the knowledge of all truths about your relationship. The Holy Spirit is the third person in the Holy Trinity; God the Father, God the Son, which is Jesus, and God the Holy Spirit. There are many attributes of the Holy Spirit. One of the many attributes being that he will teach us all things and will guide us into all truth. As we listen to the Holy Spirit, we will not live in darkness but be well prepared with the necessary knowledge to face the situations that are to come in our lives, including marriage.

> *But the Helper, the Holy Spirit, whom the Father will send in my name, he will teach you all things and bring to your remembrance all that I have said to you.*
> *John 14:26*

We need God the Holy Spirit to teach us all things and reveal those truths, known or hidden, about our relationships. How do we gain access to God the Holy Spirit, you might ask? The answer is through prayer. The most basic definition of prayer is "talking to God." Before you get married, you need to develop a strong prayer life. There are so many benefits to a strong prayer life. One benefit of a strong prayer life is that it allows you the opportunity to develop a deeper relationship with God, so that you will be able to recognize his voice when he talks to you. Just as a crying baby can be soothed and stop crying when mother is near. Due to the close bond the mother and baby have, mom's presence and voice is enough to bring security and comfort. Similarly, we need to be able to recognize God's voice when he speaks to us and the only way to do that is to spend time with him in prayer.

> *My sheep hear my voice, and I know them, and they follow me: John 10:27*
>
> *But when he, the Spirit of truth, comes, he will guide you into all the truth. He will not speak on his own; he will speak only what he hears, and he will tell you what is yet to come. John 16:13, NIV*

Before I got married, when I prayed, I would either hear an inner voice, God the Holy Spirit, say something audibly or I would feel a strong urge from the Holy Spirit to move in a certain direction. When it came to my relationship with my ex-husband, it was not that I didn't hear the Holy Spirit speak to me about the relationship. I heard Him. The problem was I chose to override His voice. With God, we have an option of listening to Him and obeying or not listening to Him. God made us free will agents with the power to choose. He won't force us to obey Him. The key is to choose to listen to His voice and follow whatever the directive is to do. When you don't follow God, you suffer the consequences.

For me, one of those consequences was a failed marriage. I remember before I got married, so many times questioning whether the relationship with my ex-husband was worth all the toxic drama we experienced. My ex-husband and I lived in a constant cycle of breaking up and getting back together. We broke up so many times because we both knew something was not right about the relationship, but then we would get back together because we both overrode the red flags for our own reasons. I don't know my ex-husband's reasons, but I know one of my reasons was I wanted to get married before thirty years of age and I loved him. As a result, my heart would not allow me to listen to the voice of the Holy Spirit within me that said to wait and accept the truth I heard him say about the relationship.

People often say, "the heart wants what the heart wants" and that is true. However, this is not the end of the matter, even our heart must align with the will of God. Another benefit of prayer is it allows us the opportunity to align our will with God's will for our lives. We need prayer for God to reveal the truths; the good, the bad, and the ugly about our relationships. Once the truths are revealed, we then must choose to use the information to align with his purpose for the relationship. The purpose could be to result in marriage, or the purpose could be to become a learning experience preparing you for the next relationship, which could be marriage. Those things are revealed by God in prayer as to what His will is for our lives. Listening to God's warnings in prayer and obeying them will help you navigate all areas of your life, including marriage.

Call unto me, and I will answer thee, and show thee great and mighty things, which thou knowest not.
Jeremiah 33:3

God knows all things including the inner most hidden places of a man's heart. How easy it is in this day and time to be deceived, so you must turn to God in prayer for the answers regarding the relationship. Deception in a relationship can involve behaviors such as making vague or ambiguous statements, telling half-truths, withholding important information, minimizing key facts, or telling outright lies. I remember a story from this older woman who told me how she was in love with a guy, but they were in a long-distance relationship. She said they would talk on the phone for hours and he would often express how he would do anything for her telling her all the things she wanted to hear. If they got married, she told him she would be willing to move to his state to be with him and he said he would do the same.

One day during the relationship, she became extremely ill. Now the idea of moving to another state was difficult because her specialty doctors were located in her home state. Besides that, if her health turned for the worse, she wanted to be near family who could help take care of her. However, if they were going to be in a relationship long term, he was going to have to be the one that moved to her state instead of her moving to his. She told him he would need to move for them to be together long term and then suddenly, he stopped calling as much. They eventually broke up because the truth was, he was unwilling to move even though he had expressed to her that he would do anything for her. Her heart was broken, and she was extremely disappointed. Eventually, she forgave him and moved on with her life.

A year later, out of the blue, he called back. In an instant, she remembered how much she loved him and how much she missed their long conversations. He convinced her he had changed and wanted to restart their relationship. So, she agreed and opened her heart up to him again because she was lonely. Months into the relationship, her health had gotten worse than it was before. So, she approached him again concerning him moving to her state so they could be together. Since he said he had changed, she thought he would have a different response. Unfortunately, he did not. He responded that he was still unwilling to move to her state and be there for her. As such, they broke up again and her heart was broken again.

As she was telling me this story, she said, "Something told me to not give him a second chance." Well, I knew that something was the Holy Spirit. The Holy Spirit warned her not to open her heart to him a second time, but she overrode that prompting by him. Now, she is dealing with the effects of a broken heart yet again. Although the Holy Spirit will answer you if you call, the key is to listen to him and obey what he says to do. If not, you open yourself up to being deceived by the enemy that comes to steal, kill, and to destroy you.

The thief cometh not, but for to steal, and to kill, and to destroy: I am come that they might have life, and that they might have it more abundantly. John 10:10

The passage above speaks of "life more abundantly." The abundant life is God's best for us. However, it is the enemy's job to steal the abundant life from you by keeping you forever bound in dysfunctional cycles such as: brokenness, depression, anxiety, and emotional pain. When your heart is involved and you love someone, these cycles can be very hard to break. You need to allow the Holy Spirit to advise you on how to break the cycles in your life, so you can be free to be with the one God has chosen for you to marry.

When it comes to cycles, the enemy will use whoever or whatever to keep you bound in cycles, and that includes but is not limited to your family, friends, co-workers, or even your spiritual leaders. No one's voice on Earth should be higher or greater than God's voice in your life. Not big mamma, not your best friend, not your high school coach, not even your favorite Sunday school teacher. Again, no one's voice should be higher or greater than God's voice in your life. Unfortunately, I made this critical mistake when I allowed the voice of a spiritual leader in my life to be greater and higher than God's voice in my life. Before I got married, I didn't realize that you could make a spiritual leader an idol. An idol is anything you love or value more than your obedience to God. An idol can be a person, image, object, or thing.

> *Thou shalt have no other gods before me. ⁴ Thou shalt not make unto thee any graven image, or any likeness of any thing that is in heaven above, or that is in the earth beneath, or that is in the water under the earth. ⁵ Thou shalt not bow down thyself to them, nor serve them: for I the LORD thy God am a jealous God, visiting the iniquity of the fathers upon the children unto the third and fourth generation of them that hate me. Exodus 20:3-5*

Our God is a jealous God. His voice is the only voice in the earth that matters. At the end of the day, a spiritual leader is still a man or a woman, which means they are not perfect. The only one that is perfect is God. Spiritual leaders can be wrong like anyone else. Whether unintentional or not, bad advice is bad advice. Be careful who you let speak into your life, especially when it comes to your intimate relationships. That is why a spiritual leader's voice should never be greater or more important than God's voice in your life even if they say, "God said" before every statement when they speak to you. Now, don't get me wrong, because He is God, God can speak through anyone, including our spiritual leaders. However, it is a sign of control and manipulation whenever a spiritual leader advises you with the "God said" before every statement without giving you the freedom to accept or reject that statement since they say it is coming from God.

The purpose behind this behavior from the spiritual leader is to undermine your ability to hear God and make judgments for yourself because the voice of the manipulative spiritual leader becomes greater than God's voice. I found this to be true when I listened to this spiritual leader advising me, I often questioned within myself saying, "Why does God only reveal truths to them about my life and not me?" This is not adding up correctly. However, I used to believe that whenever this spiritual leader would say "God said such and such," I would accept it as truth, because sometimes things worked out as they said.

The problem was I found myself going to this spiritual leader first for guidance about my life before I went to God to inquire of Him. Then, if I went to God the Holy Spirit in prayer and heard different guidance from Him, I would override what the Lord was saying, because I already accepted the spiritual leader's guidance. But as it turned out, who I needed deliverance from was that spiritual leader! In the aftermath of that confusion my mind needed to be renewed, so I could live in God's perfect will and not the will of this spiritual leader. No longer will I let a spiritual leader's voice speak louder than God's voice concerning the direction and wellbeing of my life.

My process of deliverance took years. First, I had to physically separate myself from this spiritual leader's daily influence and control. I had to set boundaries on my personal time. I no longer allowed them to have access to certain areas of my life as well as, I no longer was so easily available whenever they called. Second, I had to increase my prayer life spending more quality time with God in prayer, so I would know God's voice for myself strengthening my own relationship with him. Third, I had to get into the Word of God for myself and I started committing his scriptures to my heart. I needed to know what the Word of God said about the different areas of my life and my future. Fourth, I learned the power of declaring and decreeing the Word of God over my life.

> *Thou shalt also decree a thing, and it shall be established unto thee: and the light shall shine upon thy ways.*
> *Job 22:28*

From a biblical perspective, a decree is an official order or proclamation made by a person in authority. As such, I used my authority as a child of the most high God to decree his promises over my life. Do you know what God has promised you? If not, I would encourage you to take the time to search the Scriptures and you will find many promises that God gives to those who love and follow Him. A promise is a covenant or declaration that one will do exactly what they say they will do. I know God promised me restoration, so I began to decree and declare by mouth restoration to every area of my life using the Word of God.

Below, I listed my top four scriptures that I decreed repeatedly during my process of deliverance:

> [17] *No weapon that is formed against thee shall prosper; and every tongue that shall rise against thee in judgment*

> *thou shalt condemn. Isaiah 54:17*
>
> *I shall not die, but live, and declare the works of the LORD. Psalm 118:17*
>
> *And we know that all things work together for good to them that love God, to them who are the called according to his purpose. Romans 8:28*
>
> *May the LORD, the God of your ancestors, increase you a thousand times and bless you as he has promised! Deuteronomy 1:11, NIV*

Lastly, I went on a spiritual fast in private and renounced every idol in my life. A fast is abstaining from *food* for a period of time while seeking God's face for His direction and intervention in your life. I put a special emphasis on food because fasting is not abstaining from the use of social media or abstaining from doing your favorite activity for some time. Although doing such things can help you fine-tune your focus on God, the true meaning of a fast is abstaining from food for a while. Fasting provides an opportunity for you to increase your spiritual sensitivity and strength where your spirit man grows strong while your flesh is weakened. During my fast, I prayed to God the Holy Spirit to help guide me through this process of deliverance. I asked that He expose the truth regarding this spiritual leader's true intentions towards me. I no longer wanted to be in denial. I needed the Lord to show me a path forward free from their manipulation and control.

The Bible is full of examples of people who have abstained from food to seek answers from God. Jesus fasted in the wilderness 40 days and 40 nights to draw near to God for help.

> [1] *Then was Jesus led up of the Spirit into the wilderness to be tempted of the devil.* [2] *And when he had fasted forty days and forty nights, he was afterward an hungred.* [3]

And when the tempter came to him, he said, If thou be the Son of God, command that these stones be made bread. ⁴ But he answered and said, It is written, Man shall not live by bread alone, but by every word that proceedeth out of the mouth of God. ⁵ Then the devil taketh him up into the holy city, and setteth him on a pinnacle of the temple, ⁶ And saith unto him, If thou be the Son of God, cast thyself down: for it is written, He shall give his angels charge concerning thee: and in their hands they shall bear thee up, lest at any time thou dash thy foot against a stone. ⁷ Jesus said unto him, It is written again, Thou shalt not tempt the Lord thy God. ⁸ Again, the devil taketh him up into an exceeding high mountain, and sheweth him all the kingdoms of the world, and the glory of them; ⁹ And saith unto him, All these things will I give thee, if thou wilt fall down and worship me. ¹⁰ Then saith Jesus unto him, Get thee hence, Satan: for it is written, Thou shalt worship the Lord thy God, and him only shalt thou serve. ¹¹ Then the devil leaveth him, and, behold, angels came and ministered unto him. Matthew 4:1-11

Jesus teaches us an important lesson in the process of deliverance and that is to not agree with the devil and to answer the devil quickly with the Word of God. After my fast, God revealed to me that I had agreed with and had given power to a prophetic word spoken over my life that was not the will of God. I did not realize it before. This prophetic word was literally causing destruction to my future. I will never forget my day of deliverance. I found myself in a showdown with this spiritual leader, a Goliath-like figure in my life, sitting in this restaurant listening to them hurling all sorts of accusations against me trying to get me to come back in agreement with their prophetic word. I remember after every accusation hurled saying, "No, I don't agree, I don't receive that." They eventually got so frustrated and mad at my new response, that they got up, stormed out of the restaurant, and out of my life. Not to be heard from again.

Immediately thereafter, God sent ministering angels to me like He did Jesus in the wilderness through my local church, who prayed for me and ministered deliverance to my life. They encouraged me that God's plans for my life are good, not evil, and that His plans could not be thwarted. Through a lot of prayers and tears, once I took a stand against the enemy, I was finally free. It was not until I came out of agreement with that prophetic word and renounced the power that I gave that prophetic word to operate in my life, was I able to be finally free from it. I kept hearing God's voice in my spirit repeatedly saying, "You're Free." So, I began to confess and decree, yes indeed, I'm Free. I'm Free. I'm Free! For those of you reading this book, please be encouraged because you can be free from the enemy's plans and stay free too!

CHAPTER FIVE
Sex

One major tactic the enemy uses against singles before they get married is sex. Well, let's talk about sex, baby. First, sex is not a bad thing. God designed sex to be a good thing enjoyed by a man and a woman within the confines of marriage. Sex outside of marriage is a sin and the wages of sin is death. Meaning, engaging in sex outside of marriage opens the door for the enemy to have legal access to destroy every area of your life because God will judge the sin.

> *Marriage is honorable among all, and the bed undefiled; but fornicators and adulterers God will judge.*
> *Hebrews 13:4*

Fornicators are those who have sex outside of marriage. Adulterers are those who are married that have sex with someone that is not the their spouse. Although the world has normalized having sex outside of marriage, having sex outside of marriage is a sin the enemy can exploit and use to keep you bound into a life of sin and destruction. Why, might you ask? Because sex outside of marriage can cloud your judgment about the relationship causing you to lose the ability to hear God's voice clearly, to ignore red flags, and to be over accepting of certain bad behaviors for the sake of the relationship. To have sex legally in the eyes of God, you need to be married. Don't get me wrong, when you are in a romantic relationship, it is normal to feel those sexual desires about your partner, but you must learn how to control that sexual passion and set boundaries with your partner for the overall good of the relationship.

I remember hearing a story from a guy that was very active in the ministry serving God. Before he got married, he had dated his wife for several months and he felt like they shared common interests and goals. One night she came over to his place for dinner and they started fooling around which led to sexual intercourse. Then sex became a regular occurrence. Since he was active and out front before the congregation, he started feeling guilty. To ease his conscious he reasoned, "I am already having sex with her, so I might as well marry her."

Years later, they were headed to divorce and to a consultation at my law office. I asked him, "Would you have married her had you not had sex with her before marriage?" His response was a resounding, "No." His answer was interesting to me because I knew he was not alone. Sex is the master bait used by the enemy to destroy our relationship with God. Many people make the mistake of settling in marriage to someone who is less than what God has for them because they were having sex, or they were wanting to have sex legally in the eyes of God.

Although wanting to have sex is a natural human desire, God will give you the grace necessary to abstain from having sex while you are single if you maintain a desire to be pure in His sight. It all starts with your mindset. The battle to remain sexually pure is in our minds. Before I got married, I was a virgin. Why might you ask? Because growing up I did not want to have to worry about some of the potential consequences of sexual intercourse like pregnancy or sexually transmitted diseases. I had too much to accomplish in my life becoming this high-power attorney, so I abstained from sex completely. Also, I truly wanted to give my virginity as a gift to my husband once we got married. Somehow, I thought being a virgin would grant me some special honor with my husband and with God that would shield me against the possibility of divorce because I did it the "right" way. Well, please know it did not grant me some special shield! I still got divorced. Nevertheless, instead of some special shield, I believe God desires for us to preserve our virginity to close the door to the enemy having a legal right to have access in our lives as well as, protect us against ungodly soul ties. Having sexual intercourse with someone ties your souls together. This is called a soul tie. A soul tie is an emotional and spiritual connection between two people that is established after sex that binds them together physically, mentally, and spiritually. When soul ties are at work, you can often hear someone say when describing their relationship, "every time I try to leave this person, something keeps pulling me back to them." What is that feeling that I can't let them go even though I know I need to let them go? It is a soul tie, and ungodly soul ties need to be severed.

Although I was a virgin when I got married, that still did not mean I was a saint. I still fooled around sexually outside of marriage. Somehow, I convinced myself that my fooling around sexually with my ex-husband was not so bad with God since it was not sexual intercourse, and we were planning to get married anyway. Well, I was wrong there too. Fooling around sexually with your partner, oral sex, masturbation, and any other sexual act including but not limited to sexual intercourse outside of marriage is a sin. I can remember so clearly every time the relationship with my ex-husband was at its worst, a sexual act would occur between us, and it would reel us right back into thinking the relationship could work. Sex was the perfect lure used by the enemy to trap us in a relationship that was not right for either of us. If you are currently engaging in a sexual relationship outside of marriage, you should know that you are not alone. Many of us have fallen short by engaging in sexual activity outside marriage, so do not feel guilty, ashamed, or condemned. When I think about an example of not being condemned due to sexual sin, I think about the story of the woman taken in adultery in the Bible.

> *And the scribes and Pharisees brought unto him a woman taken in adultery; and when they had set her in the midst,* [4] *They say unto him, Master, this woman was taken in adultery, in the very act.* [5] *Now Moses in the law commanded us, that such should be stoned: but what sayest thou?* [6] *This they said, tempting him, that they might have to accuse him. But Jesus stooped down, and with his finger wrote on the ground, as though he heard them not.* [7] *So when they continued asking him, he lifted up himself, and said unto them, He that is without sin among you, let him first cast a stone at her.* [8] *And again he stooped down, and wrote on the ground.* [9] *And they which heard it, being convicted by their own conscience, went out one by one, beginning at the eldest, even unto the last: and Jesus was left alone, and the woman standing in the midst.* [10] *When Jesus had lifted up himself, and saw none but the woman, he said unto her, Woman, where are those thine accusers? hath no man condemned thee?* [11] *She said, No man, Lord. And Jesus said unto her, Neither do I condemn thee: go, and sin no more. John 8:3-11*

Just like the woman taken in adultery, you too are not condemned by God or put to shame for engaging in sexual sin. God loves you and He just wants you to repent from your sexual sin and sin no more. The good news is that you can stop engaging in sexual activity with your partner right now and repent to God. Repent is more than just shedding tears at the altar in church and saying, "I am sorry," it means true transformation in your mind and actions to not do that sin any more. To transform your mind, you must start by deciding that you will not, under no circumstances, have sex outside of marriage. That decision in your mind is the foundation from which all your future actions will derive.

To transform your future actions, you must start by actively disengaging in all forms of sexual activity. This may mean for you not staying alone in secluded or intimate places with your partner or engaging in cohabitation with your partner. This may mean for you avoiding listening to certain songs on the radio or watching certain television shows or movies that have a sexual nature or undertone. This may mean for you avoiding reading certain romantic novels, pornographic magazines, or scrolling on certain social media websites that have a sexual nature or undertone. This may mean for you avoiding sexting, talking dirty, or using other erotic communications with your partner. Whatever it means for you, repent in your mind for doing that sexual sin and in your actions do the sexual sin no more. I know that repentance may seem like a daunting task in the moment, but I am a living witness, God will give you grace to abstain from having sex while you are single. If I can do it, so can you. At the end of the day, we should want to present our bodies pure and holy to God and to man during our season of singleness.

> *Therefore, I urge you, brothers and sisters, in view of God's mercy, to offer your bodies as a living sacrifice, holy and pleasing to God—this is your true and proper worship.* Romans 12:1, NIV

This scripture is so powerful as it speaks to a person's choice to sacrifice fulfilling their own natural human desire for sex as an act of worship to God. Sacrifice means giving up something you want to do. Please know that no one is saying it is easy to abstain from having sex when you are single. Especially, given the world we live in that glorifies sex and inundates us with sexual images and content everyday, because sex is used to entice people. This is why the world says, "sex sells." Notwithstanding all the good-looking people we see walking around daily. Believe me, I understand it is not easy to abstain from having sex outside of marriage. But it becomes an easier pill to swallow when you realize abstaining from sex outside of marriage is worship to God. Worship is defined as expressing your love, reverence, and admiration for God. How amazing it is for us to know that God would see our obedience in abstaining from sex in our single season and be pleased. There is no greater joy that you can feel other than knowing that God is pleased with you. It is as if God whispers in your ear, "well done, my child."

Even if you have had sex outside of marriage, you can, and you should commit yourself to remaining sexually pure from this day forward. In essence preserving yourself for your future marriage partner. Instead of viewing your single season as a punishment, you must view your single season as a time of preparation for your future marriage partner. When I think about an example of a preparation process, I think about the story of Esther in the Bible. Esther was chosen to undergo a twelve-month preparation process of purification prior to being able to go before the King and possibly be chosen by him as the next Queen.

> *Before a young woman's turn came to go in to King Xerxes, she had to complete twelve months of beauty treatments prescribed for the women, six months with oil of myrrh and six with perfumes and cosmetics.*
> *Esther 2:12*

Myrrh has been used throughout history as an essential oil used in medicine to heal and treat certain inflammatory diseases. The first six months of Esther's preparation process was for healing and purification of her physical body. Once they were certain she was healed and pure on the inside, they spent the next six months maximizing her beauty on the outside with perfumes and cosmetics. The outcome was not just a physical change to her outside appearance, but a change from within that shined outwardly as it is stated in scripture that she found favor with the king.

> *And the king loved Esther above all the women, and she obtained grace and favour in his sight more than all the*

virgins; so that he set the royal crown upon her head, and made her queen instead of Vashti. **Esther 2:17**

The idea being conveyed in Esther is that healing and purification on the inside precedes beautification on the outside. Meaning, you can wear all the make-up you want, wear all the fancy designer clothes you can afford, and still be ugly because you are walking around full of unforgiveness or some other sin. You must take the time in your single season to prepare for your future marriage partner. This is done by eliciting the help of the Holy Spirit in prayer to guide you into all areas of truth, so you can have the knowledge necessary to work on healing and purifying the inside. Cleansing from unforgiveness, rejection, bitterness, and hurt to name a few as well as remaining sexually pure.

Any person that does not respect your choice to remain sexually pure before marriage or makes you feel pressured to have sex with them is not the marriage partner that God has chosen for you. I would confidently say run for the hills away from them as fast as you can and don't look back. The man or woman whom God has in store for you will respect your desire to be sexually pure and should demand the same from you. Settling for anything less is a recipe for disaster. Once purification on the inside is accomplished, beautification on the outside is required. If Esther spent six months in her preparation process maximizing her beauty on the outside to attract the King, why would we think as singles we can attract a high-quality partner with little or no effort to maximize our physical appearance on the outside.

Your single season is the optimal time to shed those unwanted pounds and get physically fit, which may mean for you going to the gym or changing your eating habits. Your beautification process may mean getting your teeth fixed and professionally cleaned or trying new cosmetics, perfumes, or colognes. Your beautification process may mean updating your wardrobe or changing your hairstyle. Whatever it means to you, do it. I had to. No one wants to spend the rest of their life in a marriage to someone they find physically repellent. Unless they settle, of course, which is a recipe for divorce.

CHAPTER 6
The Unexpected Aftermath of Divorce

Those who settle for less than what God has chosen for them often end up in divorce. Divorce is not always as easy as going to the attorney's office, signing the divorce paperwork, and hearing the Judge say those words, "as of today you are divorced." Although many of my divorce clients would say they felt a sense of relief upon hearing the Judge say those words, after they finished exhaling, they still had to deal with the consequences of their divorce. Yes, there are consequences to divorce. Divorce is a complicated and emotional process that can have both positive and negative consequences at the same time. Before I got married, I wish I would've known there were unexpected consequences of divorce.

FINANCIAL CONSEQUENCES

There can be positive and negative financial consequences when it comes to divorce. Many couples, when they get married, often join their finances into joint checking and savings accounts. When a divorce happens, usually the general rule is those assets get split 50/50, no matter which partner earned most of the money during the marriage to place into those accounts. In my practice as a divorce attorney, I will often sit across from couples and must explain, even if they don't have joint checking accounts, whatever money is earned during the marriage gets split 50/50 no matter who was the primary breadwinner, which includes retirement accounts, mutual funds, and other investment accounts. You can imagine the shocked looks I get from people in my office who think whatever they earn personally during the marriage is their money.

I remember having a conversation with one guy that came into my office for a consultation regarding a divorce. Although his wife worked making a modest salary, he was the primary breadwinner during the marriage making at least a six-figure salary a year. As the primary breadwinner, he was the one that made sure all the household bills were paid, which was necessary in this marriage because the wife was a compulsive gambler often spending her entire paycheck at the casino. To keep the household bills paid, they agreed to have separate checking accounts. When I told the husband the general rule is whatever is earned during the marriage gets split 50/50, whether it is in a separate account or not, all I can remember him saying is how he thought that result was so unfair because he was the one that earned the most money between them to deposit into the accounts. He was the best steward of the money between them, and if she got fifty percent of his hard-earned money, she was only going to gamble it away at the casino. So, my response to him was I am sorry, divorce is not fair.

When you think about it, it is not fair to be building this life with a person one day to having to start over another day and build a new life without them. When I say building a life, in financial terms, I am talking about examples like buying a house or car together or starting a business venture together. When divorce happens, those kinds of assets must be divided by the courts equitably between the two people. You can't practically split a house or a car in two, so how courts usually do it is they determine what the fair market value is of the assets. Once that value is determined, any debt on the assets is then deducted, and if there is any equity remaining, the parties would split that equity 50/50.

To pay the equity remaining of a house, the house may have to be sold to make sure each party gets paid their fair share, which can be a traumatic experience for many people. Why, might you ask? Because the family home can hold sentimental value that can be worth far more to the individual than what the house is monetarily worth. Often, the family home is seen as a place of comfort and familiarity, so it can be hard for couples going through a divorce to agree on which person should be ultimately awarded the home, which person should move out of the home temporarily while the divorce is pending, or whether the home should be sold in the first place. Now, to sell the family home may mean for one individual starting over living in an apartment or for another individual moving in with their parents or another relative until they can financially recover. Both choices are not ideal but are often the realities of couples transitioning through the divorce process.

Another financial consequence couples must consider after divorce is support alimony. Support alimony refers to payments made by one spouse to support a former spouse to maintain their standard of living after a divorce. Support alimony can come into play when one spouse worked during the marriage and was the primary breadwinner and the other spouse didn't work at all during the marriage for whatever reason. The other party could have been a stay-at-home parent or an individual suffering from a disability that prevented them from working during the marriage. Even after the divorce is over, the court may order the spouse that makes more money to pay support alimony for years to the spouse that makes less money to help that party maintain the same lifestyle they had during the marriage. Meaning, it is possible for a person to be forced to be financially tied to a person that they are no longer with physically for years. Yes, there serious and many cases unimaginable consequences to divorce. Divorce can bring out the worst behavior in people, especially when money is involved.

> *For the love of money is the root of all evil: which while some coveted after, they have erred from the faith, and pierced themselves through with many sorrows.*
> *1 Timothy 6:10*

As a divorce attorney, I have seen the love of money cause individuals to actively hide large sums of money from their partners, so the Judge wouldn't divide the assets. Many times, these parties will deposit money into bank accounts in other people's names or try to transfer title to certain assets, before they file for divorce, to other people's name, only to have them transferred back after the divorce is final. I have also seen people hide physical assets from the other party like a special piece of jewelry or heirloom and not divulge the location of those assets even with the threat of being held in contempt of court.

When it comes to the love of money, nothing surprises me about how evil and deceptive people can act toward each other to protect assets when going through a divorce. I remember one couple that came into my office to sign initial paperwork for an uncontested divorce. The husband wanted a divorce, but the wife was hesitant because she deep down in her heart did not want a divorce. Now, this couple throughout their marriage, had acquired a marital home, multiple empty lots, bank accounts, and numerous retirement and mutual fund accounts. During the consultation, the husband expressed to me, outside the presence of his wife, major concerns about the general rule regarding a 50/50 distribution of the assets after the divorce.

However, the wife was more concerned about saving the marriage because she loved her husband. In his conversation with her, I watched the husband convince her if she just signed the divorce paperwork with the 90/10 property distribution that he wanted, they could still work on saving the marriage, go to counseling, and possibly not even finalize the divorce. However, he knew he had no intention of keeping those promises once the divorce paperwork was signed. Eventually, she signed divorce paperwork which included a property division that basically left her with pennies compared to what he would be awarded which was all the major assets. I sat there watching them thinking how the love of money can cause people to actively deceive those they say they love; those who at one time exchanged vows. That is why I would say to anyone, please always read and seek to understand the fine print before you sign anything no matter who is telling you to sign lest, you be deceived.

Another financial issue I see often as I work with couples going through a divorce or separation is the issue of child support. During a divorce, when children are involved, the courts are going to usually order for one party to pay the other party child support for the financial support and benefit of the children. In my state, there is a mathematical formula that calculates the amount of financial support owed by a party using the combined parent's gross monthly income, parenting time, daycare, and insurance costs, and it spits out a number for one parent to pay depending on which parent makes more money and parenting time. The purpose of the computer formula is to take out issues of ambiguity on what is owed and is supposed to make things fairer across the board on how child support is calculated.

However, I have seen the love of money cause individuals who had a higher paying job before the divorce quit that job once the divorce was filed, and either work a much lower paying job or work under the table in secret to avoid paying a higher amount of child support. I have also seen individuals work a job every day and as soon as the child support agency finds out about their job and starts withholding child support out of their check, they immediately quit that job and search for a new one. Then when they get the new job, they stay on the new job only until the child support agency finds out about the new job before they quit again. It becomes a continuous cycle of job hopping to avoid paying child support.

As a result, many individuals find themselves in a position where they need to spend thousands of dollars to hire an attorney to find the money. It goes without saying but navigating the legal process can be both time-consuming and very expensive when money is at issue. As a divorce attorney, I have seen people spend thousands of dollars to hire attorneys to fight over the silliest of things just to cause hurt to the other party or spend thousands of dollars to hire attorneys to make sure the other party would not walk away from the divorce with more than a dime because of hurt. Remember the adage that hurt people hurt people, but when it comes to money that statement can be intensified.

Now, even though there are negative financial consequences to divorce, there also can be positive financial consequences to divorce as well. That husband I mentioned earlier who divorced his wife with the gambling problem, I was able to advise him that in the long run he would have more of an opportunity to improve his financial stability than staying with her. In his marriage, the wife would not only spend all her money at the casino, but she would also run up high balances on credit cards to support her spending habits. Some credit cards he knew about and some credit cards she received in secret and didn't let the husband know she had.

As we were going through the divorce process, we uncovered that the wife had managed to run up $30,000.00 in credit card debt. When divorce happens, the general rule is not only do the assets of the marriage get divided 50/50 but also all debts that are incurred during the marriage get divided 50/50. These are debts that are known and unknown by the other party. The husband found himself now fifty percent responsible for $30,000.00 in credit card debt after the divorce that he knew nothing about. Another time I remember hearing him say the words divorce is not fair. Nevertheless, I advised him on how to see the light at the end of the tunnel. Once he repaid his percentage of the marital debt after the divorce, the never-ending hole of marital debt that his ex-wife was leading him down had stopped, and he could finally look forward to a future independent of her bad spending habits and become financially stable. Still, not a situation anyone would want to sign up for, which is why it is so important to take the time and do your due diligence on your potential spouse before you get married, so you may identify red flags like bad spending habits that may not be beneficial for a successful marriage.

FAMILY CONSEQUENCES

When you get married, you not only marry your partner, but you marry their family as well. What I didn't fully realize before marriage was that not only did we have expectations for our marriage, but our families had expectations for our marriage as well. In my family, I have one brother and one sister. Before I got married, my brother always talked about how he looked forward to having a great relationship with his brother-in-law, because it was like having the brother he always wanted to have growing up. When my divorce happened, my brother was extremely hurt not only for me, but also for himself because now this dream of having this great relationship with his brother-in-law was dead and gone. My mother not only hurt for me, but also for herself because she always talked about how she looked forward to spoiling the grandchildren, and now after the divorce she no longer gets to see that dream fulfilled from that relationship. I could give countless examples, but the bottom line is I would never want any of my family members to be hurt by my decisions, yet they did hurt after my divorce and now they too needed to be healed.

When a divorce happens, there is a breach in the family unit. Navigating the new family dynamic can be a challenge for most divorced couples, especially when children are involved. In my practice as a divorce attorney, I see divorced couples fight over issues involving children every day. Fighting over issues like which school district the child will attend, how much parenting time each parent gets to spend with the child, which parent will make the primary decisions regarding the child's medical needs, or how much each parent will pay in child support. Although the best interest of the child is the legal standard courts abide by, many parents lose sight of that legal standard when going through divorce because their emotions are at an all-time high. It is not uncommon to see parents use their children as pawns or weapons against the other parent to try to gain some advantage during the divorce process. Often, a child can be made to feel in the middle of two warring parents. It is sad to see a child having to choose one parent they love over another parent they love because the parents are unwilling or unable to communicate due to their past hurts from their relationship, but it happens.

There was one time I remember attending a divorced couple's child's event. Although both parents were present to celebrate the child's accomplishment, neither parent spoke to the other parent at the event. I watched both parents actively try to avoid getting near each other in the space designated. Standing on opposite sides of the room. Never addressing the child at the same time. When the child took pictures at the event, the child took pictures with mom's side of the family in one area and then took pictures with dad's side of the family in another area. The child sees all of this going on and understands exactly what is happening between their parents. It was truly sad for me to watch this young child not just be allowed to be a child, but having to mediate between their two parents and manage each of their parents' emotions during the party by making sure both sides were happy and okay. In situations like this, healing and forgiveness is needed for everyone to move forward because the children are often the forgotten ones who face consequences too in a divorce.

One such negative consequence of divorce or separation is the child loses the benefits of what God intended for an intact family unit to provide for a child. God's design for the family unit can be found in the Bible. After God created Adam, the first man, God observed that it was not good for him to be alone, so God created Eve from Adam's rib, forming the first union of marriage.

> *The LORD God said, "It is not good for the man to be alone. I will make a helper suitable for him." [19] Now the LORD God had formed out of the ground all the wild animals and all the birds in the sky. He brought them to the man to see what he would name them; and whatever the man called each living creature, that was its name. [20] So the man gave names to all the livestock, the birds in the sky and all the wild animals. But for Adam no suitable helper was found. [21] So the LORD God caused the man to fall into a deep sleep; and while he was sleeping, he took one of the man's ribs and then closed up the place with flesh. [22] Then the LORD God made a woman from the rib he had taken out of the man, and he brought her to the man. [23] The man said, "This is now bone of my bones and flesh of my flesh; she shall be called 'woman,' for she was taken out of man."[24] That is why a man leaves his father and mother and is united to his wife, and they become one flesh. Genesis 2:18-24*

God's concept for marriage is for the two people to become one flesh. This is a spiritual concept meaning the two people (husband and wife) becoming one mind, one will, and one emotion unified in marriage to achieve God's purpose on the Earth. From this initial act of creation, God intended for a man and woman to come together in marriage to form the foundation of the family unit. The family unit, according to God's design, is meant to be blessed by God to provide love, support, and companionship to all those within the family unit. This family unit serves as a place free from physical and emotional abuse where individuals can find love, security, comfort, joy, peace, safety, and acceptance.

> ***And God blessed them, and God said unto them, Be fruitful, and multiply, and replenish the earth, and subdue it: and have dominion over the fish of the sea, and over the fowl of the air, and over every living thing that moveth upon the earth. Genesis 1:28***

One such purpose of the family unit as stated in scripture is to be fruitful, multiply, and replenish the earth. In the confines of the family unit, as it is intended by God, children are to be raised, taught morals and values, and guided towards a life of purpose and meaning. An intact family unit can provide a child with stability because we have two parents in the same household unified in their decisions regarding the upbringing of the child. When a divorce happens, the two people (husband and wife) that were one flesh according to Scripture revert to becoming two flesh. Now, there are two parents in two different households with two different minds, two different wills, and two different emotions parenting the same child as before. It's not uncommon to see in one parent's home, the child is subjected to a parenting style with high expectations and clear standards. While in the other parent's home the child is subjected to a parenting style with low expectations and few rules.

For example, at mom's house, the children can stay up until midnight on a school night scrolling social media. At dad's house, the children must put the phones away and go to bed at 8:00 p.m., on a school night. Same child but two different households. Many children find it hard to thrive mentally between two homes when there are different parenting styles and no consistency between the households. Often these children experience symptoms of depression and anxiety. You may see these symptoms manifest in children having suicidal thoughts or self-harming behaviors such as doing illegal drugs or having an eating disorder. Although every situation and every child are different, the point is to not settle before marriage to try to avoid this situation altogether for the children because it was never God's intent for the family unit to be divided.

The world has made divided family units or co-parenting outside of marriage appear easy and even glamorous when it is not. Co-parenting is the shared parenting of a child by their parents who are not married or living apart. Often you hear these celebrity couples issue public statements when they are separating saying things like, "Although we regret to announce that we are legally separating, we will always be the best of friends and we look forward to being the best co-parents ever," like co-parenting outside of marriage is some prize to be achieved. Co-parenting outside of marriage is no prize. I often hear my divorce clients tell me how hard co-parenting is because they must make a real effort to put aside their own feelings of hurt and pain toward the other parent to put the well-being of their child first.

Many parents express the challenges they experience from seeing their child every day to now seeing that child only half the amount of time because the child's time must be shared with the other parent or express how hard it is for them to make decisions for a child with someone that has completely different ideas, goals, and parenting styles. Many co-parents also find it especially difficult when the other parent starts a new relationship with someone else, and now that new person has feelings and emotions that need to be managed as they will partake in the responsibilities of raising the child. It can be a mess, but it takes mature adults to set aside their feelings of hurt and pain and put the children first.

Co-parenting can also present a challenge if the co-parent is a narcissist, which is a person who has excessive interests or admiration of themselves, or an emotional or physical abuser. Boundaries need to be established to help parents co-parent with these types of individuals. In cases of high-conflict relationships or abusive marriages, separation or divorce will provide a safer and more stable environment for children. Children who live in that type of environment often experience emotional turmoil, adjustment issues, and other stress-related traumas witnessing their parents' conflict during marriage and even after divorce. The legal process can help provide parents with those necessary boundaries through a parenting plan and other court orders to ensure the safety of all individuals involved. That is why it is so important not to choose to just have a child with anyone, you need to exercise due diligence with the person you choose to be the biological parent of your child. If you don't exercise that due diligence, you and everyone connected to you will face the consequences, whether they are expected or not.

EMOTIONAL CONSEQUENCES

Going through a divorce can trigger all kinds of troubling, uncomfortable, and frightening emotions, including but not limited to shock, grief, loneliness, anxiety, fear, depression, guilt, anger, and frustration. Even after the divorce is finalized, some individuals may struggle with these challenging emotions for an extended period. After my divorce, I know I was not prepared to experience the array of emotions mentioned above, and I even struggled managing these emotions in my daily life. Some days I would feel extremely sad and guilty for the failure of the marriage. I would say things like, "How did I let this happen,' or "Why couldn't I just figure out how to make it work." Then, other days I would feel extremely angry at God and my ex-husband, and I would blame them both that the divorce happened. I would say things like, "How can God be so good when He didn't fix my marriage," and "It was all my ex-husband's fault."

Then, other days I would feel fearful about my future and feel so lonely that I would desire to be back in a relationship with my ex-husband. I would say things like, "What if this was my one and only chance to get married," and "Maybe things with my ex-husband were not so bad that we should try again." I found myself vacillating continuously between periods of extreme sadness to periods of extreme anger to periods of extreme loneliness. It was not uncommon to find myself during the day just crying uncontrollably and many times being unable to fully understand to articulate why I was crying.

One emotion I didn't fully understand and particularly didn't expect to experience was grief. Grief is usually defined as *the mental anguish experienced by someone after a significant loss, usually the death of a loved one*. It is easy for most people to associate the emotion of grief with when a loved one passes away because you lose a relationship with them due to their death. You lose the opportunity to hear their voice or to speak to them ever again. You lose the opportunity to feel their loving embrace or to share new memories with them, which is emotionally painful. It is natural to understand that you would miss your loved one and as a result, you would grieve their loss since you will never see them on Earth again. However, when it comes to divorce, the emotion of grief is not as easy for most people to associate with divorce. Yet, grief is a natural reaction to divorce because it too is also a loss of the relationship.

The only difference is the loved one is still alive, not dead, and you will likely see them on Earth again, especially if you have children together and must co-parent. Even if children are involved, after divorce, you still lose the opportunity for companionship, shared memories outside of the children, and emotional support from that individual like the way it was when you were in a relationship. To not grieve the loss of the relationship, you run the risk of not healing completely. After a divorce, I have seen people jump immediately into a new relationship without grieving the last relationship, and those people usually repeat the same mistakes from the last relationship and hurt the new people in the new relationship. Remember *hurt people hurt people*. That is why grieving a divorce is so vital to the healing process to move forward to the best God has in store for you.

Weeping may endure for a night, but joy cometh in the morning. Psalm 30:5

This scripture suggests that while you may experience grief after divorce for a period, joy will eventually come. As such, you must give yourself the freedom to grieve the relationship and the grace to experience each one of the emotions mentioned earlier. Then, as you are experiencing the emotions, you must not beat yourself up for how long the grieving process takes because each person's period of grieving is different depending on the circumstances. Someone whose marriage was betrayed through infidelity or abuse might take an individual longer to grieve than someone who has watched their marriage deteriorate for years. While any of these emotions mentioned earlier can feel immobilizing at first, the key is not to give up hope in God that you will see better days where you become stuck and can't move on.

If you ever find yourself stuck in your emotions, there is no shame in seeking the services of a licensed therapist to help you talk and work through processing those emotions. I know therapy can still be taboo in our culture, but I would recommend therapy to anyone who desires help in processing their emotions. After my divorce, I sought help from a licensed therapist, and I found the therapist gave me a safe place to talk out my hurt emotions with no fear of judgment and with the protection of confidentiality because sometimes you just can't tell certain friends and family your business. The licensed therapist was able to help me gain perspective on my marriage and divorce that I used to move forward. Divorce then became an opportunity for personal growth and self-discovery. Remember divorce is not just an ending to a relationship, it is an opportunity to learn from your past mistakes, begin again by exercising the due diligence necessary to make better decisions, and create a brighter future for yourself.

CHAPTER SEVEN

Curses

A part of exercising due diligence is seeking to uncover what curses may be operating in you and your partner's lives. Before I got married, I wish I had known that curses were real. A curse is a supernatural force designed to bring harm and destruction to a person's life. There are two common types of curses: *generational curses and word curses*. These curses can have a significant effect on the success or failure of a marriage, so it is important to know what curses may be in operation in your marriage, so you and your partner can agree in prayer to break them.

GENERATIONAL CURSES

Generational curses are sin patterns passed down through family bloodlines that give demons legal access to cause destruction in your life. This type of curse is attributed to past actions or transgressions from past family members and is thought to bring about continuous misfortune, harm, affliction, and destruction to subsequent family members until the curse is broken or resolved. The Bible speaks of generational curses in the Book of Exodus.

> *Then the LORD came down in the cloud and stood there with him and proclaimed his name, the LORD. ⁶And he passed in front of Moses, proclaiming, "The LORD, the LORD, the compassionate and gracious God, slow to anger, abounding in love and faithfulness, ⁷ maintaining love to thousands, and forgiving wickedness, rebellion and sin. Yet he does not leave the guilty unpunished; he punishes the children and their children for the sin of the parents to the third and fourth generation."*
>
> *Exodus 34:5-7*

There were generational curses on my family's bloodline and on my ex-husband's family's bloodline. Though we were oblivious to their existence these generational curses were in operation during our marriage causing destruction and division between us. In my family, going back four generations on my father's side, my father had been divorced before he married my mother. My father's mother and father divorced. My father's mother's mother had been divorced. So, even though I grew up in a healthy two-parent married household, the door of sin was opened through divorce in my bloodline, which meant my marriage could face the consequences of my family's past sins. Because my ex-husband and I never had the conversation about his family lineage going back four generations, I am unaware fully of all the sins that were on his family's bloodline. However, there are patterns of sin from his family's generations that I observed.

In my ex-husband's family, his mother and father had divorced. At the time we married, all his male siblings had conceived children in sin through fornication and had never been married. My ex-husband was the first male sibling to get married and he had no children outside of marriage. Given the sin of divorce and fornication was present in our bloodlines, the enemy had a legal right to attack our marriage causing it to face the consequences of our family's past sins. Soon after I married my ex-husband, bad things would happen, and divorce became an immediate topic of conversation between us. Even when we were able to overcome certain obstacles and find common ground, there always felt like there was a supernatural force working against us causing us both to feel like we had one foot in and one foot outside the door of the relationship.

The objective of one of the generational curses that was at work in our marriage was for my ex-husband and I to divorce, for him to enter fornication outside of marriage, and for him to conceive a child in sin outside of marriage. Thus, continuing the sin patterns for both of us on to the next generation. Well clearly, we got divorced and years after our divorce was final, my ex-husband conceived a child in sin through fornication out of wedlock like his male siblings. Had we known that we were dealing with this generational curse during our marriage, we could have taken the necessary actions to touch and agree in prayer to break the curse.

What does it mean to break a curse? To break a curse means to bring to a complete end all ill effects the curse would have on your life. Generational curses need to be broken in prayer by someone in the bloodline. After my divorce, I was determined it was going to be me, the bloodline breaker of all curses in my family because I wanted every member of my family to walk in absolute freedom. To accomplish this feat, it would have been nice to get a play-by-play of all the sins committed by my family going back four generations, but that didn't happen. It is not uncommon to find out that your family members just don't know this information or sometimes there are family secrets that span generations and getting that information from certain family members is nearly impossible. That is why it is important to seek help from the Holy Spirit to reveal these truths about generational curses to you about your family.

> *Howbeit when he, the Spirit of truth, is come, he will guide you into all truth: for he shall not speak of himself; but whatsoever he shall hear, that shall he speak: and he will shew you things to come. John 16:13*

The Holy Spirit can help guide you to identify patterns of sin on your family's bloodline. Examples of sin patterns I have heard of are all the men on the bloodline have children outside of marriage, or all the men on the bloodline cheat on their spouses. Another sin pattern could be all the women on the bloodline die prematurely at the age of 50 due to cancer, or all the women on the bloodline divorce at some time in their lives. Once these sin patterns are identified, the next step is to *repent, renounce,* and *replace* them with the Word of God every sin committed on the bloodline. Please know that these are sins that you are aware of and sins that you are not aware of. It is important to note that the Holy Spirit guiding you into all truth does not necessarily mean that you will get the exact revelation on where the door to sin was opened on your bloodline. This means that you may never know that it was great grandma that opened the door to sin on the bloodline by worshiping idols or by having pre-marital sex or by committing adultery on great grandpa. So, as a rule of thumb, it is best just to cover all your bases and repent from all sins.

Remember, repent means to turn from doing that sin and to do the sin no more. After repentance, the next step is to renounce the sin. Renounce means *to formally declare that you disown and come out of agreement or covenant with that sin.* I found myself in prayer declaring to God that I repent from all sins, known and unknown, that were committed by me and anyone else on my bloodline. I repented and renounced agreement from all sins including but not limited to the following: idolatry, fornication, abortion, molestation, incest, lying, stealing, adultery, divorce, infidelity, pride, murder, free masonry, sororities, fraternities, envy, lust, greed, gluttony, anger, unbelief, unforgiveness, and an evil covenant made with any other god.

> *If we confess our sins, he is faithful and just to forgive us our sins, and to cleanse us from all unrighteousness.*
> *1 John 1:9*

Renouncement is an important step in the process because God promises to forgive us or sins with the confession. After renouncement, the final step in the process of breaking generational curses is to replace the old ungodly covenants with new godly covenants. An example of this step can be found in the book of Joshua in the Bible.

And if it seem evil unto you to serve the LORD, choose you this day whom ye will serve; whether the gods which your fathers served that were on the other side of the flood, or the gods of the Amorites, in whose land ye dwell: but as for me and my house, we will serve the LORD. Joshua 24:15

When Joshua said those words, "as for me and my house, we will serve the Lord," he established a godly covenant to commit to the ways of God and serve God not only for himself but for all his generations. I think that is important to note here that not only can sin patterns be passed down to subsequent generations, but also godly patterns can also be passed down to subsequent generations. What pattern gets passed down depends on your choice. Joshua reminds us in this scripture that we are free will agents with the ability to choose God or to choose sin. So, I suggest that you choose to serve God today. If not, you choose to suffer the consequences of sin for you and subsequent generations.

During my process of breaking these generational curses on my bloodline, I was advised to watch these YouTube videos by Robert Henderson named *The Courts of Heaven*. Never had I realized, before watching these YouTube videos, that the enemy could have a legal right to cause delay to the promises of God in my life. The Courts of Heaven is not a prayer, but it is a spiritual dimension where legal cases are brought before God to judge. You can find a reference to the Courts of Heaven in the Book of Daniel in the Bible.

> *"As I looked, "thrones were set in place, and the Ancient of Days took his seat. His clothing was as white as snow; the hair of his head was white like wool. His throne was flaming with fire, and its wheels were all ablaze. [10] A river of fire was flowing, coming out from before him. Thousands upon thousands attended him; ten thousand times ten thousand stood before him. The court was seated, and the books were opened. Daniel 7:9-10, NIV*

My case of unforgiveness was brought by the enemy in the Courts of Heaven for God to judge. The enemy used my unforgiveness against my ex-husband as a legal right to launch a case of accusations against me in the Courts of Heaven with the sole purpose of delaying God's promises of restoration in my life. In legal terms, I was guilty as sin. As such, my guilty plea in prayer before God, the righteous Judge, was to plead the blood of Jesus over my sin. The phrase "pleading the blood" refers to the blood that Jesus Christ shed when He was on the cross that now covers our sins. When you plead the blood of Jesus, you have laid down your guilty case and put your entire confidence in the power that Jesus has over the enemy and the new covenant Jesus established between us and God that the shedding of his blood would cover a multitude of our sins.

> *He himself bore our sins" in his body on the cross, so that we might die to sins and live for righteousness; "by his wounds you have been healed. 1 Peter 2:24*

Thank God for the blood of Jesus. Once I forgave my ex-husband, renounced the sin of unforgiveness, and replaced that ungodly covenant with sin with the new godly covenant established by the blood of Jesus, did the enemy lose his legal right to accuse me in the Courts of Heaven. Only then was I able to present my case in the Courts of Heaven for full restoration in every area of my life.

WORD CURSES

Growing up as a little girl I remember hearing people singing, "Sticks and stones may break my bones, but words will never hurt me." Well, as an adult I now understand that's not the truth. Words can certainly hurt you just as much as sticks and stones. Why, might you ask? Because words can be used by the enemy against you to curse you and delay the promises of God in your life. Before I got married, I wish I had known word curses were real. A word curse is a spoken word used by an individual to speak harm or misfortune over your life. The tongue holds great power to speak life and death over your life because it can be used as a weapon to harm and destroy or as a tool to build and heal.

> *Death and life are in the power of the tongue: and they that love it shall eat the fruit thereof. Proverbs 18:21*

Because words matter, the enemy will use anyone, including those who say they love but to speak a negative word to curse your life. One thing I had to learn was to look beyond the person speaking the negative word and see that it is a spirit inside the person that is at work speaking death over your life. I am not telling you that action is something easy to do. You truly need God's grace to be able to do it. But, at the end of the day, you must love the person but hate the spirit.

> *For we wrestle not against flesh and blood, but against principalities, against powers, against the rulers of the darkness of this world, against spiritual wickedness in high places. Ephesians 6:12*

Words carry an impact, whether positive or negative, on those who are the recipients of them. What impact have certain negative words had on your life? Maybe you heard these negative words years and years ago, but you still think about them or allow them to guide your feelings, actions, and decisions today. Some examples of negative words that can be used by the enemy to curse your life are, "You will never be good enough." "You can't do anything right." "You are a failure." "You are not progressing." "You will never get married," or "no one will ever love you."

These word curses come from the enemy to get you to come into agreement with what is being said to cause death and delay to the promises of God in your life. Any way you have agreed with or accepted these negative words that were spoken over your life must be revoked. To ultimately break free from these word curses you must renounce your agreement with them. Once you renounce your agreement with them, these word curses will lose any power to operate in your life. In my process of renouncing word curses over my life, I repeatedly decreed the following scripture:

> *No weapon that is formed against thee shall prosper; and every tongue that shall rise against thee in judgment thou shalt condemn. This is the heritage of the servants of the LORD, and their righteousness is of me, saith the LORD. Isaiah 54:17*

Every tongue that spoke a word curse against any area in my life, I prayed that God condemned. Condemned is defined as *expressing complete disapproval of a thing*. Remember, word curses only have power over you if you approve and agree with them. Do not agree with the enemy's word curses and thereby render them powerless to operate in your life. Instead, express agreement with what God says about the plans He has for your life.

> *For I know the plans I have for you," declares the LORD, "plans to prosper you and not to harm you, plans to give you hope and a future. Jeremiah 29:11*

How do you express agreement with what God's plans are for your future? You start by speaking life over your situation using the Word of God. Jesus states in the Bible that man cannot live by bread alone but by every word that comes out of the mouth of God. (Matthew 4:4) The word of God is life. As such, we can use the word of God to break the power of word curses and replace them with blessings instead. Here are some powerful decrees that you can speak over yourself using the Word of God:

> 1. *Philippians 4:13: "I can do all things through Christ who strengthens me."*
>
> 2. *1 Peter 2:24: "By His stripes, I am healed."*

3. 1 John 4:4: "Greater is He who is in me than he who is in the world."

4. 2 Timothy 1:7: "God has not given me the spirit of fear; but of power, and of love, and of a sound mind."

5. Philippians 4:19: "My God shall supply all my needs according to His riches in glory by Christ Jesus."

6. Nehemiah 8:10: "I will not be sad or depressed because the joy of the Lord is my strength."

7. Isaiah 26:3: "My God will keep me in perfect peace as my mind is stayed on Him."

8. Philippians 1:6: "I am confident of this very thing that He who has begun a good work in me will complete it."

9. Romans 8:28: "All things work together for my good, because I love God, and I'm called to his purpose."

10. Ephesians 3:20: "My God is able to do exceedingly abundantly more than I can ask or thing, according to his power that is at work within me."

Now, I would be remiss if I didn't acknowledge the fact that I was not speaking these powerful decrees 24 hours a day 7 days a week after I got divorced. There were many days I didn't decree anything positive at all. It was not uncommon for thoughts of doubt to creep into my mind. I found myself thinking, "Will God really do it for me?" I often wondered if a godly marriage was in the cards for me. Especially when the years passed me by and I would see people who I knew were living in sin, didn't have a prayer life, were just plain trifling to the core, and yet they were the first ones running to the altar getting married. I often asked myself, "What is this foolishness I see, why them and not me? When will God ever allow it to be my turn?"

Doubt is a real state of mind that we all experience at different times in our lives. If you find yourself in a place of doubt right now in believing what God promises for your life, please know that you are not alone. The question is not whether you will experience doubt, but rather how you deal with your doubt when it comes. A powerful lesson of this concept can be found in the Gospel of Mark. There a father brought his demon-possessed son to Jesus' disciples for help, but they could not heal him. Then Jesus arrived, and the father begged Jesus to heal his son saying, "If you can do anything, have compassion on us and help us."

> *²³ Jesus said to him, "If you can believe, all things are possible to him who believes." ²⁴ Immediately the father of the child cried out and said with tears, "Lord, I believe; help my unbelief!" Mark 9:23-24*

"Help my unbelief," is a powerful prayer. We see in this scripture the father of the child's desire to immediately express faith to believe God but at the same time be genuine enough to acknowledge he had doubts. It is possible to believe in God, but also struggle with doubts in his ability to come through when you need him. Our doubts should be an indication to us that we need more faith to believe in God in whatever area in our lives where there is doubt. The closer our connection to God, the more we spend time with Him, we'll see Him working. As we become more aware of our need for Him and how He comes through for us in the different areas of our lives, our faith will strengthen.

You may have heard of that adage, "He may not come when you want Him, but He will be there right on time." God will do what He said He will do. The good news is that our doubts have no impact on whether God will do something for us. If you continue reading the passage of scripture, you will find that Jesus healed the boy despite the father's unbelief. Remember, God can do it and He will for those who love Him. What areas of your life are you struggling to believe in God that He can and will do it for you? For singles, it is not uncommon to doubt that God can and will divinely connect you with your spouse. Especially when the years pass by, and you see no real prospects. Believe me, I understand your pain, but I implore you to wait on God and never stop expecting your heart's desires to manifest.

Take delight in the LORD, and he will give you the desires of your heart. Psalm 37:4 NIV

If you desire a godly marriage, have the faith to believe God for it, and then wait on Him to manifest it at the right time. Remember, faith is the substance of things hoped for, the evidence of things not seen. Meaning, you may not see your spouse now, but believe God that one day you will see your spouse and that the godly marriage you desire will manifest. This is true even if you have been divorced. Divorcees, you are not disqualified from seeing the promises of God manifest in your life. Even though I am still walking this process out, please know I stand in faith believing God for all of you who desire a godly marriage that God will make it happen for you.

CHAPTER EIGHT
Final Thoughts

When I heard God tell me to write this book, I waited for some time to start writing it because I wanted the book to have a certain happy ending. How I envisioned my final thoughts would start by saying how I triumphed after my divorce, met the man of my dreams, fell in love, and was having his baby. But, ugh no. That didn't happen before I finished writing the book. Instead, what happened was a shift in my perspective on how I triumphed after my divorce. No longer am I seeking a romantic relationship to validate my victory. I am victorious with or without it. Why, might you ask? Because despite my divorce, my relationship with God is intact, and I am still seeking his face first in all things concerning my life.

> *But seek ye first the kingdom of God, and his righteousness; and all these things shall be added unto you. Matthew 6:33*

Your relationship with God is paramount; before the marriage, the kids, and the business, its God. The enemy thought after my divorce that I would give up on that relationship, curse God, and die. However, I thank God today that He loved me enough not to leave me in my sins. It was God's grace and mercy that kept me, so I wouldn't give up. Looking back, I realize that I am not that same naive girl that chose to settle in my romantic relationships. I now want more for my life and I pray you want more for your life too. At the end of the day, marriage is a beautiful thing, especially when you allow God to orchestrate it from the beginning to the end. I have been fortunate in my life to see beautiful God-ordained marriages, so I know they exist, and I believe they are obtainable not only for me but for you too.

While writing this book, I often thought of my Goddaughters, and what I would advise them in dating before they got married. How I would hope they would read this book, learn from my mistakes, and make better decisions than I did in their romantic relationships. I truly hope my testimony will help not only them, but you too.

> *And they overcame him by the blood of the Lamb, and by the word of their testimony; and they loved not their lives unto the death.   Revelation 12:11*

As I said earlier, God had a different happy ending for this book. I am finally not ashamed to write it, so here is my testimony. I'm 41, divorced, and still single, but I am no longer willing to settle for less than God's best for me. I may not have my godly marriage yet, but I have increased my faith enough to trust God's timing to wait on him to orchestrate when and how it will happen for me. With God being in control, I believe that all things are possible. God promised me restoration and He promised to give me the desires of my heart. So, I choose to believe God this day and decree and declare that restoration is coming to every area of my life. Today, I know my value in God as his daughter, a wife, a mother, a minister, and a Judge. My life is a work in progress. I end this book finally saying that I am open and ready to receive the best God has for me. Hopefully, after reading my book, you will be able to say the same for your life! God Bless!

The End

ABOUT THE AUTHOR

JESSIKA MICHELLE TATE is the daughter of Buddy and Darlene Tate. She was born and raised in Tulsa, Oklahoma, where she graduated from Booker T. Washington High School, class of 2000. In 2004, she received a bachelor's degree in business management at the University of Oklahoma. She later received her Juris Doctorate at the University of Oklahoma School of Law.

In 2009, she started the Tate Law Firm, where she specializes in custody, divorce, guardianship, and personal injury. Jessika has a passion for helping members of her community, especially those who are often underrepresented at the courthouse, gain the legal and personal knowledge necessary to navigate the complexities of the legal system successfully. You can find out more details about the Tate Law Firm at www.jtatetulsalaw.com.

In 2012, Jessika was married and later divorced, wherein her journey of discovery and healing began. Also, in 2021, a career milestone occurred when she received an appointment as an Associate Municipal Judge, where she has presided over the needs of the citizens of the City of Tulsa in her courtroom ever since. In addition to her distinguished career in law, Jessika also attends and serves in ministry at Kingdom Church in Broken Arrow, Oklahoma. Although Jessika has come through many trials and tribulations, today, she is walking in victory and is using her life story as a living testimony that there is life after divorce.

ABOUT THE PUBLISHER

Let Life to Legacy bring your story to literary life! We offer the following publishing services: manuscript development, editing, transcription services, ghostwriting, cover design, copyright services, ISBN assignment, worldwide distribution, and eBook conversion. Throughout production, we keep the author informed every step of the way. Even if you do not have a manuscript, that's not a problem for us. We can ghostwrite your book from audio recordings or legible handwritten documents. Whether print-on-demand or trade publishing, we have packages to meet your publishing needs. At Life to Legacy, we take the stress out of becoming a published author. Unlike other so-called publishers, we do more than print books. Our books and eBooks are distributed to book buyers, distributors, and online retailers throughout the world—this is real publishing! Call us today for a free quote. Please visit our website:

www.Life2Legacy.com

or call us

708-272-4444

Send e-mail inquiries to

Life2Legacybooks@att.net

www.ingramcontent.com/pod-product-compliance
Lightning Source LLC
LaVergne TN
LVHW091315080426
835510LV00007B/503